Loris—
With respect
for all that you hold,
& all that you give!
Keep Loving!
Kim

Crossing the Owl's Bridge

A Guide for Grieving People
Who Still Love

Kim Bateman Ph.D.

 CHIRON PUBLICATIONS • ASHEVILLE, NORTH CAROLINA

www.ChironPublicatons.com

978-1-63051-372-6   Paperback
978-1-63051-373-3   Hardcover
978-1-63051-374-0   ebook

Cover design and typesetting by Danijela Mijailović
Printed in the United States of America.

Library of Congress Cataloging-in-Publication Data

Names: Bateman, Kim, 1964- author.
Title: Crossing the owl's bridge : a guide for grieving people who still love
    / Kim Bateman Ph.D.
Description: Asheville, North Carolina : Chiron Publications, [2016] |
    Includes bibliographical references and index.
Identifiers: LCCN 2016011748 (print) | LCCN 2016019810 (ebook) | ISBN
    9781630513726 (pbk. : alk. paper) | ISBN 9781630513733 (hardcover : alk.
    paper) | ISBN 9781630513740 (E-book)
Subjects: LCSH: Grief. | Bereavement. | Love.
Classification: LCC BF575.G7 B378 2016 (print) | LCC BF575.G7 (ebook) | DDC
    155.9/37--dc23
LC record available at https://lccn.loc.gov/2016011748

Dedicated
to

Elisabeth Harris Hathaway
April 23, 1962-May 23, 2015

and

Chad Murray Bateman
March 28, 1968-March 15, 1990

Who taught me (albeit painfully) the beauty of presence in absence.

Acknowledgements

My gratitude to the teachers: North Tahoe High School English teacher Barbara Koenig Roberts, who gave us structure and form for our voices; Sierra Nevada College professor Laird Blackwell, for reflecting his students' particular soulfulness, thus lighting the fires; and my first teachers — Linda Burdick (Mom) and Lee Bateman (Dad).

I also want to acknowledge the work of Greg Mogenson, who wrote "Greeting the Angels." His book influenced my ideas regarding loss and laid the foundation for this book. And Juliet Erickson, who believed in its value.

Note to the Bereaved

More than anything
I wanted to heal you

To dip my hand
Into the icy, raging river
Of your pain

And draw out polished stones

One by one.

K. Augustus (Poem 12, 2015)

Table of Contents

*"Your absence has gone through me/
like thread through a needle/
Everything I do is stitched with its color."*[1]

W.S. Merwin

Introduction

I was afraid that if I let go of my remaining brother's hand, he would dissolve into the monochrome gray wash of the murky images of my imagination, and then another tangible third of me would be gone. We were in the back seat of a car on the way to view the body of our brother. Our mother had stayed on the couch of our childhood home, clutching the manila envelope that contained all the things Chad had in his possession the moment he was taken over a 750-foot cliff by a wall of snow while extreme skiing—Carmex, a brass ring that his girlfriend had made him, some change, a thread friendship bracelet, and a lighter. In the numb haze of that moment, it struck me as surreal that you could have a whole, vibrant person with you one day and the next have a few items and icy stillness. She had been crying in the low, guttural animal tones that only a mother who has lost a child can make. Our father wasn't speaking. It was

---

[1] "Separation" by W. S. Merwin, collected in THE SECOND FOUR BOOKS OF POEMS. Copyright © 1960, 1961, 1962, 1963, 1964, 1965, 1966, 1967, "sion of The Wylie Agency LLC.

difficult to hold these places—the raw, unmediated, pain of mother loss AND the carefully calculated, controlling denial of pain that, in this moment, was father loss. I held tightly to Scot's hand, needing desperately to keep him in the concrete world as we rounded the corner to the mortuary.

The sheriff explained that the cause of death was "blunt force trauma," not suffocation. He meant this information to be reassuring, in that we didn't have to imagine him falling that far or trapped under snow. Still, the image of him at the bottom of that cliff with all his bones broken was too much to hold. I thought of all the times that Chad had broken his bones when he was young, and how doctors always remarked about how strong he was and how quickly he would heal. I knew that this time, there would be no colorful designs on casts, or wire hangers stretched to scratch underneath the plaster. There would be no healing, it seemed, for any of us. Grief, as I would learn, is its own special form of madness.

When Chad's body was broken by snow and pointed rocks, our family life, relationships, and most carefully constructed senses of self also shattered. Before heading back to our respective lives in New York, Boston, Humboldt County, and Lake Tahoe, we stood at the base of Munchkins Chutes and looked up the line that he had chosen to ski that day. Our father said, "madness," and I wondered if perhaps it was "suicide." Scot just shook his head, and our mother, well, she just cried. And cried. She is still crying. I felt tortured by questions— "Who was he … really?" and "What was the significance of his life?" "Where is he now?" "Is he?" "How do I keep loving someone who is no longer physically here?" And echoing in my heart were the unarticulated, yet pressing, whisperings, "Who am I … really?"

and "What is the significance of my life?" "Where am I now?" "Who am I separate from the loving of my beloved?" The familiar hook upon which I had hung my coat of identity was no longer there, and the pain was unbearable.

From a psychological perspective, many grief theorists see the bereavement process as one of "letting go" of something that no longer exists.[2] The ultimate goal of therapy is to stop feeling attached to your loved one and reinvest your energy in new people, projects and activities. It is well intended but misses the point completely. We want to talk to our loved ones. We crave their responses. *We still love.* It is like the person who loses a limb and continues to receive sensations from it. Others may not be able to see it, but they can still feel its presence.[3] We are not alone in this pursuit. The desire to become informed by and be in contact with the deceased appears in every culture throughout all of recorded history.[4] The Egyptians and Indians believed that they could see the image of the departed in a blob of ink. The Maoris and ancient Greeks saw faces in drops of blood. The Pawnee Native Americans consulted their dead

---

[2] John Bowlby, "Process of Mourning," *International Journal of Psychoanalysis* 42 (1961): 317-340; Sigmund Freud, "Mourning and Melancholia," in *Collected Works, Vol. 4,* ed. J. Riviere (New York: Basic, 1917/1959), 154 ; George H. Pollack, "Process and Affect: Mourning and Grief," *International Journal of Psychoanalysis,* 59 (1978): 267; Lorraine D. Siggins, "Mourning: A Critical Survey of the Literature," *International Journal of Psychoanalysis,* 47 (1966): 14-25; Harry Sullivan, "The Dynamics of Emotion," *Clinical Studies in Psychiatry* (New York: W.W. Norton, 1956), 91-127.
[3] Robert Romanyshyn, "Hosting Ghosts" unpublished lecture (Pacifica Graduate Institute, Carpinteria, CA, March 15, 1998).
[4] Colin Parkes, Pittu Laungani, and William Young, eds., *Death and Bereavement Across Cultures* (New York: Routledge, 1997), 233-243.

ancestors in a bowl of water, and the Nigerians studied the ripples in a pond for messages from beyond. Similarly, in Siberia, Tungas shamans or medicine people gazed into copper mirrors to connect with the deceased. Some tribal people actually use the skull of the deceased person as a pillow in the hopes of receiving divine wisdom from them.[5] In both ancient and contemporary times the bereaved are attracted to psychics, mediums, and channelers. We are still seeking relationship.

The strict voice of psychoanalytic "science" would say that this attempt at communication is all a misguided attempt to hold on to a "lost object."[6] Any contact with the dead is seen as a form of "wish fulfillment,"[7] we hope for something with so much intensity that our mind is helping us by creating it. This may be part of the story, but something tells me (a ghost, perhaps) that there is so much more.

About a year into my own grief process, I came across a Japanese proverb that said, "My barn having burned to the ground, I can now see the moon." This image introduced me to the idea that we do have to say goodbye in the material. But, we can also look at it as an invitation to say hello to a different type of relationship.[8] As I began looking around at different cultures, and particularly their stories, I found that this theme of the loss of the physical coupled with a continued relationship in the

---

[5] Patricia Garfield, *The Dream Messenger* (New York: Simon & Schuster, 1997), 40.

[6] John Bowlby, *Attachment and loss: Loss, Sadness and Depression, Vol. 3.* (New York: Basic Books, 1980), 38-40.

[7] Freud, "Mourning and Melancholia," 160.

[8] Greg Mogenson, *Greeting the Angels* (New York: Baywood, 1992). See this book for foundational theory in imaginal mourning.

imaginal is ubiquitous. This idea will be used to give you tools to create the symbols or rituals that you need to create a bridge—a bridge between you and your loved one, and perhaps also between the current place of pain to a more developed, richer, connected sense of self. We may not be able to fix the suffering, but we can change it through giving it meaning. Through folk tales and examples, this book will show how you can *still love*.

Why Folktales?[9]

As soon as a tale begins, maybe with "In olden times when magic still helped," or "when animals could still talk," or "a long, long time ago, in a faraway place," it signals a departure into the symbolic, and we know that something vague, unarticulated, and hidden will soon be revealed. Fairy tales offer external symbols that reflect the complex topography of the collective imagination. Hedges of thorns grow around sleeping castles, little girls are swallowed by wolves, and heroes and heroines become caught in labyrinths both external and internal. Unwary travelers are smashed between rocks or swallowed by whales. A loyal wife weaves and unravels a beautiful cloth, waiting for her husband to return. And a disturbed woman combs the depths of the river with her sticklike hands and her long hair, trying to retrieve the souls of the children she had drowned while she wails and wails.

---

[9] For more on psychological applications of fairy tales, see the work of Marie-Louise von Franz, Marion Woodman, Robert Bly, Verena Kast, Clarissa Pinkola-Estés, Bruno Bettelheim.

Through the tensions they create, we are offered mirrors of our own dynamics, clear expressions of our emotions, and pathways through our angst. In death we are faced with the most profound of existential questions and folktales present us with these dilemmas on a regular basis—a king must decide which of his three sons is most worthy to inherit his kingdom, a poor man must find a godfather for his 13th child, a motherless child has no shoes. The story promises to unveil pathways through these issues. Bad things happen in folk stories—the baby dies, the brother goes blind, the girl gets her hands or feet cut off, true love doesn't always prevail, the wicked end up getting rewards. We feel right along with the characters and at the same time are giving expression to our own unnamed emotions. And we learn important truths. In *Beauty and the Beast*, we see that you must be loved before you can be lovable.[10] As Cinderella sits in the fireplace, sorting the lentils and peas from the ashes, we know that sometimes life is about serving systems and people who are not rational and figuring out what can sustain you (lentils, peas) and what cannot (ashes). We learn that faith, and a little bit of pixie dust, goes a long, long way. No one has to tell us these things, we are shown them and ultimately see for ourselves.

Through all these tensions, there is an underlying safety in this rhythm, this holding, as the story lines show us that something deeper is at work. In grief, our yearnings and pain feel vague and unarticulated. It is hard to imagine our loved ones

---

[10] Bruno Bettelheim, *The Uses of Enchantment* (New York: Vintage Books, 2010), 62.

without their bodies. It is even harder to imagine ourselves without them. Grief, like a fairy tale, is a place where logic and linear time are suspended. Our desires are hidden but familiar, distant yet ever present, dark and compelling. Our feelings are chaotic, formless, shifting, potently present and then dissolved, only to return again with steely sharpness. Our loved one has evaporated and our emotions feel just as fuzzy. The stories help us to concretize both our loved one and our sense of self. They help us understand that we can usher the image of the deceased from the abstract, back to the concrete, and ultimately, release it back to the abstract, all while connected through the invisible lifeline of love.

Many folktales show us pathways through grief. Nyctea of the Pacific Northwest is a particularly wise one.

Few people have seen her, but those who have caught a glimpse by the full moon say she is as wide as she is tall with bare feet that curl like roots going into the ground and hands more like talons than fingers. She has long, greasy-gray matted hair that is tied up in vulture feathers and mossy breath. Her eyes are large and fixed in their sockets and the noises that she makes are more bird than human—tchkt, tchkt, caw, tchkt, tchkt, caw. And she is followed by birds who hope she will know them.

They call her Nyctea, which means, of the night, and she lives in the hollowed-out stumps of redwood trees that have been hit by lightning. It is there that she collects treasures of the forest—snail shells, and mushroom caps, lichen, and bits of fox fur. But the most coveted treasures of all are owl parts which are the bones, translucent/hollow, light as a grain of rice, but strong as the wind, the talons, the feathers. And when she has gathered all the bones of a particular owl and puts them in the order an owl's bones should be, she harvests earth from the seasonal creeks and she very carefully and lovingly forms the shape of the creature, thinking as she does this of the nature of that particular bird. And when the clay dries, and she needs to mold it she uses the salt water truth of her tears to ply it, leaving sockets for wide eyes and putting the claws back in place. And while she is doing this she sings softly, as a grandmother would to a child, and through the breath going in and out, in and out, which creates the rhythm of her song, she warms the clay which slowly gives way to flesh, and feather, and heartbeat. And when her song is finished the owl opens its yellow/green eyes, spreads its wings and flies, equipped now to cross the "owl's bridge" to the next realm, leaving a downy feather or two and the quivering memory of its beauty in the dank, wet air.

Nyctea can show us much about the grieving process. In deep pain, we instinctually return to night consciousness, and our animal-like senses become heightened through the need to survive. We symbolically grow talons with which to claw ourselves out of the psychological hole. The world of day consciousness, or rational thought and normal functioning, seems very far away, and our primary task is to gather and reconstruct both our loved one and our sense of self. We are searching for and collecting that which has been lost in this world—metaphorically gathering bones. When a loved one dies, we are denied the physical person, but we continue to have access to them through our memories, dreams, and imaginations. It is compelling that though physically not there, the deceased become psychologically more present. We search our mental databases for examples of things they've said and done. We gather pictures and belongings. We smell their clothes, eat their favorite foods, and listen to their music. Rooting through my brother's things, every word he'd written seemed suddenly important. We wanted to wear his hats. And the small pin that said "Just Visiting This Planet" seemed a numinous premonition. It was a strange fiasco with friends and family vying for something (anything) to serve as a physical reminder of the person whom no one could believe was gone. We told stories about Chad at the party after the funeral, and 20 years later, we continue to perform psychic excavations into our memories, both individually and with each other. Loved ones may no longer be present in physical reality, but they are developing a strong presence in our psychic or imaginal realities. Like Nyctea, we are gathering and reconstructing as a way to piece together the lost person and create meaning. We are making his-story (or hers). And as we do so, it is important to use our tears, our pain, to help sculpt the particular soulfulness that is the image of our loved one and reflect the complexity of our relationship.

And what about the singing over bones part? Nyctea reminds us that in the quiet moments of attending to our relationship with the deceased, there is the ancient cycle of breath beneath it all. In life we take in and we let go, and she tells us to use this rhythm as the foundation for the song you will sing— the one that will sing up new life for your loved one and yourself in the process.

As a clinical psychologist and one who has taught courses in death and dying for almost 20 years, I have witnessed some people metaphorically "singing over bones." In our town, a woman lost her 18-month-old son in a tragic car accident. A couple of months later, when she was in the most jagged places of her grief, she reread the sheriff's report, which indicated that an unsecured car seat may have contributed to the fatality. This woman set up car seat checkpoints once a month. People would line up for blocks, and she would put her bony knee (she was a very tiny woman) into each car seat and she would pry and pull and tug on that seat belt until it was secure. She said that every time she pulled on a seat belt, she was loving Luke.

I also worked with a 6-year-old girl who had lost her mother to breast cancer. Her father was beside himself, and she also felt responsible for her 4-year-old brother. When I was talking with her, I said, "Tell me about your mother, what did she love?" And she said, "Mama loves TEA!" It was her idea to set up a tea party every Sunday and set a place for her mother at the table. After a few months, even her father joined in, and to this day, it is a meaningful ritual for her. When she wants to talk with her mother, she sets an empty tea cup across from herself.

There's also the story of the woman from Chicago who lost her husband after many years. Because he had been the one to drive, she decided she would walk or take the bus anywhere she wanted to go. It was on her walks that she started noticing single gloves lying on the ground. There was something about those gloves that resonated very deeply with her because they were useless and discarded without their mates. And so she began collecting them, taking them home and stuffing them in the dresser. And when the dresser was overflowing, she got out her husband's old ladder and put it up against the tree in the back-yard and hung each glove by fishing line. She said that when the wind blows, they all wave together, and it is as if they are "waving good-bye and waving hello" —what a lovely way of characterizing transitions.[11]

These bereaved people have taken the image of the deceased from the abstract and made it concrete. Like Nyctea, they have mindfully formed something physical through which to still love. She shows us that we can use our relationship with the deceased to create the rituals that keep us in connection. And as we feel more comfortable with our loved one symbolically present, like Nyctea, we also intuitively know that we must allow them to continue on their own journey. We come to realize that the dead have a fate beyond our own tears and that we, too, will follow them across the "owl's bridge" someday. The love, however, doesn't fade—we find new ways for its expression.

Since the loss of my brother, each new death of a loved one feels like a fresh hell, as I struggle to make sense of the senseless. With humility, I must admit to being confounded by death, but also recognize that I am being drawn into interplay between the concrete and the abstract, and a profound awareness of something much larger, and more universal—the hope that love is more powerful than death. Though I still struggle, I have learned that it may be through physically losing someone that we are offered the opportunity to actually discover them and ourselves. "Not only do we see our loved ones in their wholeness after death; we see ourselves through their eyes."[12] Seen this way, death presents an extraordinary opportunity for a deepened relationship.

---

[11] Susan Taylor, "Waving Good-bye and Waving Hello," in *Inside Grief*, ed. Line Wise (Incline Village, NV: Wise Press, 2001), 60-63. Reprinted with permission from Wise Press.
[12] Mogenson, p. 71.

1

A Map of the Metaphorical Tasks

Like Nyctea, who serves as a wise guide in the difficult but fertile places of loss, there is a Tlingit tale that sets up a series of metaphorical tasks for the bereaved. These two stories are used throughout this book to demonstrate foundational psychological themes, with other worldwide tales woven in to accentuate salient points. Though the tasks are described in a linear fashion, it can be envisioned as more of a spiral, with patterns that repeat while the psyche still moves forward. Thus, the bereaved might find themselves back in earlier states, like raw pain, or anger, though the work of the psyche is still going on, albeit subtly. I heard something close to this version of the Tlingit tale[13] from a storyteller around a campfire at Malakoff Diggins, in the foothills of the Sierra Nevada Mountains.

---

[13] Tlingits are indigenous people of the Pacific Northwest. A written version of this folk tale was retrieved from http://www.sacred-texts.com/nam/nw/tmt/tmt065.htm on 11/5/15. From John R. Swanton, (Bureau of American Ethnology Bulletin 39, 1909)

The Image that Came to Life

A long time ago, in a place that is far away, but not so far away called the Queen Charlotte Islands, there lived a young chief who was very much in love with his wife. But shortly after their wedding celebration, the bride, with cheeks the color of salmon and hair as dark as the deepest part of the ocean, became ill. Her eyes, which were as reflective and wise as Raven herself, glazed over and the chief approached shamans near and far. He sent his best canoes to ease and hasten their journey. But to everyone's disappointment, their help and healing was to no avail. The young woman became increasingly ill and on a moonless night the Great Spirit came and gathered up her last breath and she died.

The young chief mourned deeply over the death of his wife. In intense pain, he went to all the surrounding villages and asked their best woodcarvers to carve a statue of his wife. He needed to have her there with him, and he spared no expense in commissioning her likeness. He told every carver all he remembered about the curve of her back, and the way her eyes creased when she was laughing. He told about the time she caught a fish with her bare hands, and how the raindrops that landed on her lashes sparkled. Still, none of them succeeded at making a statue that resembled her, and the chief fell deeper and deeper into despair.

Meanwhile, in the chief's very own village there lived a humble woodcarver. On a certain evening, this carver sat next to the young chief at the fire and said to him, "You wander from here to there asking strangers to carve your wife's image, and nobody makes anything that looks like her. I have seen your wife, and more importantly, I have seen you and your wife together. I never

22

thought I might carve her face one day, but if you let me, I will try." The chief had lost hope, but could see no harm in the effort. The woodcarver found a block of red-cedar wood, and began his work.

After much time and attentiveness, the statue was finished and the carver dressed it in clothing similar to what he had seen the young woman wear. He then invited the Young Chief to come and see his work. Upon seeing the statue, sitting there just like his wife used to, the Chief felt profoundly happy. The humble carver had reproduced her image perfectly. When the Chief tried to re-ward the carver, he refused and explained that he had undertaken the work because the Chief's sorrow had saddened him. With a bittersweet sense of satisfaction, the Chief took his wife home.

As soon as the statue was home, the Chief dressed it in his dead wife's real clothes, including a very colorful robe that had seabird shapes on it. He really felt that she had returned to him, and he treated the image just as he had treated his wife. He took his small dishes of seal meat and fish by her side and talked to her about matters of the village. There were times when he awoke, curled around the woody base, having dreamed that she was really there. He still grieved greatly, and his many tears stained the wood a deeper shade of red.

One day, when he sat by her feeling very sorrowed, he felt the statue move. He thought that he had only imagined motion, but he could not help checking the image every day; he felt strongly that sooner or later it would come to life. He told others about this, and after some time everybody in the village knew of the move-ment, and people came to look at it. They too had to look closely because the statue was so real that surely it was coming to life. When a great deal of time had passed the Chief carefully touched the statue's body and it was just like a human body. Although it was a real body, the image could neither move nor speak.

A while later, the image seemed to groan from its chest, like wood buckling, and the Chief realized that the statue was unwell. He asked his brothers and close friends to help him move the statue from where it had customarily stood. It was a difficult task, in that the statue was extraordinarily heavy and seemed rooted to the place, but with great effort, they managed to shift it.

And there in the house, beneath the statue and on top of the floor, grew a small red-cedar tree. It was left there and grew to be very tall.

To this day the red cedars on Queen Charlotte Islands look beautiful. When the people see a beautiful cedar they say, "This one looks like a baby of the Chief's wife." As time passed the image of the young woman became more and more like a human being, and people came to look at it from near and far. The woman did not move much and she never spoke. But the Chief knew what the image-woman had to say. It was through his dreams that he knew she was talking to him.

This tale serves as a powerful reminder of the tasks inherent in the work of grief. It shows us the movement from the physical to the imaginal and to all the points between these places. The story begins with the introduction of the "chief" and his young wife. Developmentally, this can be viewed as a time of naiveté. Many of us are all familiar with the time before the loss of a loved one, when we lived in an unconscious state of innocence where all things seem possible. The death of the chief's wife can be seen as the moment when he is initiated into a new state of affairs, or a place that feels emotionally unfamiliar. The stage is set for the bereaved's first task, which is to move into foreign and difficult psychological territory. This period is discussed in Chapter 2 and is called Initiation.

Deep in mourning, the chief is said to search from village to village looking for a carver to create an imitation of his wife. This process may be seen as the bereaved's attempt to concretize the fading image of the deceased by actively gathering memories and information to co-author a replica of his wife. This story will ultimately become the invisible lifeline through which he connects and expresses his love. He is also searching for external models of how to fill the emptiness. Many mourners begin by reviewing religious traditions and exploring books on the afterlife. Other attempts might include filling the space of the loss quickly through relationships, projects, or substances such as sleeping pills or alcohol. This phase or task, according to the Tlingit tale, is an external searching for ideas, behaviors, people or places that will 1) solidify the image of the deceased and 2) offer models of viable ways through the confusion and pain. And like a teenager who must try on different personas to see what resonates internally with his or her developing sense of self, this phase is necessary for future growth. Though often initially comforting, the ultimately unsatisfying belief is that someone or something out there is going to be able to give the mourner something that they or it is incapable of providing, an internal sense of peace.

In the story, the chief eventually heeds the call for an enrichment of perspective and looks inward. He secures someone in his "own village" to carve a likeness of his lost loved one. This man is said to be one who has "seen" his wife. In psychological terms, the carver may be an internal aspect of one's self, as in a part of yourself that is able to quietly observe your actions and reactions. Or, the carver can be seen as an external person who truly witnesses the particular complexity of your relationship. It must be one who can authentically give credence to the image of the deceased as well as understanding the significance of the loss to the bereaved. The ongoing task is to create a place and space for the expression of your grief and to find someone to sit with you there (Chapter 3, Gathering Bones).

Though the chief is honoring the image of the deceased, he wants it to be an unchanging representation of his wife. In a way, the carving/image of the deceased is petrified because the living want the lost one to be, and react, and provide for them as they did while alive. This desire is completely understandable. A concrete enactment of the wish to hold on to the physical is the practice of stuffing beloved pets that are deceased or continuing to behave as if your loved one is alive and away on a short trip. The psychological truth here is that we want our loved ones to stay who we need them to be. We can't imagine our lives without them. The difficult task, according to the story, is to let what can no longer sustain us, in this case, and attachment to the physical, truly die. This period is unquestionably the most excruciating and can be punctuated with many tears. Interestingly, it is the expression of this profound sorrow that becomes the elixir that leads to the subsequent growth. Think of the Chief's tears watering the cedar statue of his wife. Painful feelings, navigating in the dark, and sometimes falling into that precipitous, emotional hole are the themes of Chapter 4, The Abyss. The next section, Stuck in the Abyss, presents stories that we tell ourselves that may hobble us into thinking that we will remain in the Abyss forever (Chapter 5). It points out the thoughts and feelings that can contribute to feeling "stuck" in the place of raw pain without remedy and suggests pathways through. This part shows us that breakdown can also be breakthrough.

A turning point in the Tlingit story occurs when the chief, after a long period of time, believes that he witnesses a movement in the statue. At this time, he is still deeply in grief and sitting beside, or attending to, the memory of his wife. This point may speak to the moment in bereavement when the mourner has been prayerfully nurturing the memory of the deceased and becomes suddenly aware that he or she cannot hold the person back any longer. The image of the deceased wants to be free. It becomes "unwell" if not allowed to move on. It is significant that the chief recognizes the true state of affairs and is instrumental in seeking help to facilitate his dead wife's movement. He is participating in the next task, which is allowing her image to transform (Chapter 6, Singing Over Bones). In doing so, the chief simultaneously and unknowingly gives himself permission to move. This theme in the story may be likened to the grieving mother who keeps her lost child's things exactly as they were or the widow who continues to set a place at the table for her deceased husband. These practices are comforting and helpful. But after some time, and much attentiveness, the rigidity no longer seems necessary and may impede needed movement. The loosening of these restraints allows both the living and the dead to progress.

This phenomenon can be gleaned from the sentence, "And there in the house, beneath the statue and on top of the floor, grew a small red-cedar tree." The house may be compared to our identity or sense of self, in that our homes are often reflections and expressions of our individuality, values, and style. So, there in the house—or within the bereaved, beneath the statue—or at the root of the image of the deceased, on top of the floor, which may be seen as a new ground or platform upon which the living and deceased have forged their new relationship, SOMETHING GROWS. That something, as the story relays is "beautiful," and begets more and more beauty. The creation of the red-cedar tree, which requires tears, and attentiveness to self and others, illustrates the transition to a period of rejuvenation. A physical enactment of love, often through the use of symbols, is the hallmark of imaginal connection. Note that there is no suggestion of "getting over it" or "forgetting about" the lost loved one. Instead, a different relationship is forged.

The Tlingit story ends, "But the Chief knew what the image-woman had to say. It was through his dreams that he knew she was talking to him." This paramount task involves being receptive to a dialogue that connects the mythic with the personal (Chapter 7, Crossing the Owl's Bridge). This idea takes us beyond the focus on individuals and into the world of experiencing the universal.

This book weaves the wisdom of worldwide folk tales and offers people's experiences throughout to present the anatomy of loss and offer strategies for ways through. A recurring message is that the end of a material relationship can also be seen as invitation to say hello to a different type of relationship, allowing us to still love. It will give you tools to create the rituals that you need to create a bridge—a bridge between you and your loved one, and perhaps also between the current place of pain and a more developed, richer, connected sense of self. By the end, you may find yourself feeling part of the ancient rhythms of those red cedars as they petrify and become reborn through our tending, and perhaps you will be more able to sing beyond the bones.

"Once having traversed the threshold, the hero moves in a dream landscape of curiously fluid, ambiguous forms, where he must survive a succession of trials." [1]

Joseph Campbell

2

Initiation

The first phase, according to the Tlingit tale, is moving from a place of innocence toward a place of knowledge. This initiation is communicated by the reference to the "young chief" who is on the brink of crossing into the space of loss. It is significant that he is seen as immature and referred to in lowercase letters. Later, he will be identified as the "Chief," which indicates that he has responded to the challenges that depth demands and allowed himself to sit with the mystery of life and death and sharpen his intuitive abilities.

In stories told around the world, this movement is foreshadowed by the appearance of a sign or a guide that signals that the hero or heroine is about to be drawn into a parallel world. The rabbit appears to Alice. In many Native American stories, it is the presence of Coyote, the Trickster. For some Eskimos, a black raven mysteriously flies by.

---

[1] Joseph Campbell, *The Hero with a* Thousand *Faces* (Princeton: Princeton University Press, 1973), 97.

29

Sometimes, the instigator can appear as an external set of circumstances. Aladdin is exiled in a cave. Briar Rose (Sleeping Beauty) enters a deep sleep. Little Red Riding Hood ends up in the stomach of a wolf. Or, the guide can appear in the form of inner knowing. Snow White runs into the dark and gloomy forest. Dante finds himself in a mysterious wood. Other protagonists flee of their own volition to the desert, an island, or an endless ocean. In bereavement, it is Fate itself that leads us across the threshold. It is time to leave the familiar and enter a surreal place where all logic is suspended.

One tale that aptly offers the kaleidoscope of emotions and strategies for initiation into the space of loss is a story called *The Lindworm*.[2] I heard this version from a Norwegian story-teller on the beach in Carpinteria, CA.

A long time ago, before your grandmother's time—before your great-grandmother's time, and before your great-great-grand-mother's time there lived a King and a Queen who wanted very much to conceive a child but were unable to. As hope faded and time grew thinner and thinner, the Queen, who usually conducted her affairs with the utmost in grace and decorum, did a very unqueenly thing. When the castle became dark and it seemed that even the portraits on the wall were slumbering, she crept out her window and climbed down the trellis, sprinting across the court-yard. The Queen scaled the castle wall and found herself in the

---

[2] An older, written version of Prince Lindworm appears in Peter Christian Asbjørnsen, George Webbe Dasent. *East of the Sun and West of the Moon* (George H. Doran Company, New York, 1922): 53-64.

dark and gloomy forest. There she ran into the night. Every crackle of a branch made her heart race and the thickets scratched her snowy white skin, but she was driven onward with an instinct that was not to be denied. After many hours of running, the Queen collapsed right in front of the hut of the wildish wood hag. On beholding the fearsome sight of the woman, the Queen hesitated, but at last cleared her throat and said, "I have come far to consult with you about how I might beget a child from my own loins."

The hag smacked her greasy lips and ground her sharp teeth and spat out, "Why should I help you?"

And the Queen very simply replied, "Because I ask."

"Hmmmph," groaned the hag, "That is the right answer."

The Queen is instructed to place a golden goblet upside down in the northeast corner of her garden. In a month's time, she is told there will be a red rose and a white rose growing underneath. The Queen is to eat the red rose if she wants a boy child and the white rose if she wants a girl child. Under no circumstances is she to eat both. The Queen hastens home to follow the hag's advice.

After one moon's cycle, the Queen steals away in the night to her garden and lifts the goblet. As the old woman had foretold, there are two flowers growing there. She decides that she wants to eat the red one, to guarantee her King an heir. But as she begins eating she is overcome by an insatiable desire to eat both. Though she knows she shouldn't, she can't help but eat the white one as well. As the hag predicted, the Queen becomes pregnant that night.

After nine months the Queen feels her first labor pangs and retires to her chambers. And very quickly, she feels the new heir pushing his way towards life. And as she leans over to see her new-

born as it crowns from her body, the Queen is paralyzed by what she sees. Out from her loins slithers a grotesque creature with slimy scales and sharp teeth: a serpent. The Lindworm.

The Lindworm squirms across the bed and coils down the bed-post until its belly is on the planks of the floor. A slow and guttural hissing sound ensues from its throat as it makes its way towards the door and down the hall. The Queen is completely immobi-lized, unable to make a sound.

Soon thereafter, the Queen's labor pains quicken again and as her servants arrive, she births a second child: a perfectly healthy, beautiful baby boy. The entire kingdom celebrates the King and Queen's good fortune.

The Queen is so taken with her second son that she manages to forget to tell anyone about the first. For many years the royal family lives in relative bliss, unaware of the Queen's secret of the Lindworm's presence. This innocence is shattered on the day they send the prince out to search for a suitable match for his marriage.

In a fearsome scene, the prince's carriage is stopped in the road by a large hissing serpent who demands, "He shall not have a bride until I have a bride…assss issss sssoooo." The prince returns home and tells his parents of the event and his mother is forced to confess her long held secret. The King concedes that as the eldest son, the Lindworm must be found a bride before the prince can marry.

Proclamations are sent throughout the land and the perfect princess is located and acquisitioned. She is as beautiful as she is innocent and she appears on the bridal altar in a thickly crocheted veil. It is so thick, that the princess cannot see who she is promising her life to. The vows are made and the veils are lifted…and there before her postures the hideous visage of her groom. His eyes are red and slanted. His scales are oozing pus. Rows and rows of yellowed teeth are bared. The princess-bride is stunned into silence but manages a weak, "no...." Off she is taken to the bridal chambers where the door is shut and bolted.

In the morning when the servants check the bridal chamber, they are aghast at the gruesome sight. There on the bed is the Lindworm, his gnarled teeth dripping blood. There is no princess to be found, just a crumpled up wedding gown and a soiled veil.

The Lindworm, sneering, slithers past them and says, "He shall not have a bride until I have a bride, asss issss sssssoooo."

Once again the King sends out a proclamation and once again the perfect princess is secured. She stands at the altar in a thickly crocheted veil and says her vows. Once again the veil is lifted and she beholds the terrifying sight of the Lindworm. "NO!!!" she pleads, and is carried kicking and screaming to the bridal chamber where the door is shut and bolted.

The servants open the door slowly the next morning and find the Lindworm smacking his lips, which are caked in human flesh. He slimes past and jeers, "He shall not have a bride until I have a bride, asss isss sssoooo."

By now the word of the King's eldest son has traveled about the state and it is becoming difficult to attract a possible bride for him. So the King goes out amongst his own people and happens upon a humble cobbler. Knowing that the cobbler has a beautiful daughter, the King bows deeply and requests the cobbler's daughter's hand in marriage for his eldest son. Deeply honored, the cobbler returns the bow and agrees.

Pandemonium ensues in the streets as the word is spread of the impending marriage. The cobbler's daughter is very much beloved, and the thought of her death is highly distressing. Upon hearing the news herself, she goes screaming through the streets ripping at her hair like a madwoman. She runs pell mell through the town until she finds herself at the far reaches of the uninhabited area.

As night begins to fall, the cobbler's daughter races into the dark and gloomy forest. Every twig seems to scratch her snowy white skin, every sound seems to signal certain death. She runs on through the night like this until she collapses in exhaustion in front of the hut of the wildish hag.

The wildish hag knows what has become of the girl and takes her into her home. She gives her very specific instructions as to what she is to do and sends her back to town.

Once home, the cobbler's daughter approaches the King and Queen and agrees to marry their eldest son if they consent to her conditions. She says, "One, I would like ten pure silk slips for underneath my gown. Two, I would like a whole basketful of whips to be placed in the bridal chamber. And three, I would like two tubs to be placed in our room. One should be filled with woodashes mixed with lye and the other with milk." The King and Queen agree, thinking it is some sort of strange peasant custom.

On the day of the wedding the entire village goes into mourning. The window sashes are shut and the people dressed in black. Many refuse to attend the festivities. But the cobbler's daughter has a knowing in her heart as she stands on the bridal altar and refuses to wear the crocheted veil. She looks right into the slanted red eyes of the Lindworm and does not flinch when he shows her his jagged teeth.

The vows are said and the promises made and off they are ushered to the bridal chamber. Once there, the Lindworm leans in towards her with his foul breath and says, "Take off your dressss."

And she does.

But underneath her dress is a pure white silk slip.

Angered, he says, "Take of your ssslip!"

And she replies, "Not until you take off one of your skins."

Taken aback at having been spoken to in such a way, the Lindworm does as he is told and takes off one of his skins.

And she takes off a slip.

But underneath that slip is another and the Lindworm becomes enraged. "I ssssaid, take off your ssslip!"

"Not until you take off another skin."

And he does.

And on it goes like this with his taking off a skin and her taking off a slip until all of his layers are removed and all of her slips lay on the floor.

The cobbler's daughter then picks up a whip and with previously untapped rage, begins beating the Lindworm. Without his scales or skins, he is vulnerable and his flesh opens in gaping wounds that look like little mouths.

She whips with such force that the whip breaks in half.

She picks up another whip and with all her might, beats the monster. The whip breaks and he bleeds and she picks up another. She continues until the basketful of whips is used up. And she threw them all to the side.

The cobbler's daughter then bends down and picks up the gelatinous blob of bleeding flesh and confidently places it in the tub of woodashes and lye. When the Lindworm is clean, she gathers him up very lovingly in her arms and places him in the tub of milk.

The next day, the servants wait outside the door to the bridal chamber and with great trepidation, open it soundlessly.

There in the bed lay a handsome, strong Prince holding an extraordinarily happy Princess who had been joined together in a new way. And that's how the people say it happened.

The Lindworm story is rich in archetypal imagery, and there are some dynamics that are most applicable to early stages of grief work. Imagine the monster as a symbol of the external circumstance of Death, as well as the internal ugliness that is unleashed after a loss. The ancient story can communicate exactly what must be done to negotiate through the difficult, initial period of grieving.

Though there are earlier choices that indicate a departure from the mundane, the appearance of the Lindworm is the first unambiguous signal that circumstances have moved irretrievably into a new realm. When the serpent is born, it is a pivotal moment around which the events of the future will forever revolve. As in death, attention has shifted from one state of affairs to another, and there is a crossing of a threshold. We have been catapulted into a relationship with the unknown. This unfamiliar territory is terrifying because we are leaving comfort, established emotional patterns, and senses of self. So, when Death, as the guide, shows up on our doorstep, it is a profound moment in the soul life of one who loves deeply.

Marion

It was Mother's Day 1996. I was supposed to go down to the Bay to see Jenny, but I had a sinus infection, and the doctor said I shouldn't go. So Jenny said that she and Marcia would fly up here.

Initiation

I had a strange feeling about Jenny flying to Truckee, but reminded myself to trust. Marcia's father flew them up in their small plane. Jenny had just finished her Master's in Social Work, and we were so proud of her. The day went so well.

At twilight, Sheila and I drove everyone to the Truckee Airport. We were allowed to pull our car right up on the tarmac. I remember Jenny looking at me saying, "good-bye." And that was so odd, her looking right at me and saying "good-bye" like that. The plane taxied to the end of the runway and remained there too long. I thought that something must be wrong. Finally, the plane took off and passed over the car, and the passengers were waving. And I said, "I'm not going to look because I don't want to see her crash." So I turned away and when I turned back around, I watched them crash. They made a turn sideways (to the left). If the pilot had gone straight, he would have set the plane back down on the runway. They had not gone up very far. My younger daughter, Stephanie, ran to help but I couldn't move.

Then, for a few minutes, I had perfect clarity. I can envision myself running up the tower steps and telling them that there had been a crash. I remember calling my supervisor and telling her that someone needed to cover my shift. Someone handed me Jenny's purse, and then I was at the police station.

After that, everything became a blur. The next few years can be recalled only as a dreamlike sequence, with salient experiences emerging and fading. Marion does not measure events in the time/space continuum that most of us are accustomed to. For her, life is calibrated as happening "Before Jenny" or "After Jenny." That single moment defines and colors all others.

Those who have experienced a sudden or traumatic loss can attest to this phenomenon. We can often recall, with great clarity, the events leading up to the death. It is as if time slows down, and one is able to attend to the most obscure of details. We know what we were wearing, what was said, who we were with, and what we were doing. It is much like witnessing the assassination of JFK, watching the Challenger explode, or seeing the Twin Towers go down on 9/11, only it is much more personal and intense. We find that we cannot change the channel on this particular station of suffering. We have stepped into the dream landscape, and the death itself becomes an axle around which everything else revolves.

Waylon

I was standing on the back porch looking at the lower field. I let the boys do the cutting there because it was the easiest. Not many rocks or cheat grass. Junior was operating the windrower, and the new hired hand was behind him on the baler. I watched the long, clean lines and the perfect jellyrolls of hay spitting out as they went. And there was Jarod, only 14 but following behind in the International while Max and his cousin tried to load some of the hay. The truck lurched forward just as Max was trying to jump into the back. For a moment it looked like a clown act, with him tumbling forward and all. But something caught on the edge of the back bumper. And in what seemed like an instant, but also an eternity, Max's body went limp like an old rag doll, and he was just being dragged along under the truck. I yelled and ran, but the kids couldn't hear me over the noise, and by the time I stopped them, Max was—well—just gone. You couldn't even recognize his body as a body because nothing was in the place it was supposed to be.

My wife makes me go to church every Sunday, and I can't say that I ever got it until that day. If this Jesus character was so important to them all, I can see why our calendar marks time from the day of his death. Everything just stands still, even while it keeps on going.

The loss of a dearly held treasure sets up a famine of the soul in which time and space have little meaning. Suffering keeps its own clock.

The characters in the Lindworm story have varied reactions to the crossing of the threshold and the certainty of a dreaded spiritual famine. If we examine each woman as internal aspects of ourselves, they present an anatomy of immediate grief responses. The Queen is immobilized when she first comprehends the magnitude of the monster before her. The first princess is horrified and manages to utter a "no." The second princess goes kicking and screaming. It is only the cobbler's daughter who has the gift of wildish wisdom (as bestowed by the hag) and can look with clear sight at the tasks that lie before her when the bridal chamber door is shut and bolted.

When facing the terrifying thoughts and feelings that accompany the encountering of "the monster," our egos are the first to step in to take care of us. They may shut us down, producing numbness, or refuse to acknowledge the reality of loss. They may even become enraged. One or all of these strategies may be enacted to defend against the erosion of the fragile ecosystem of the self. It is about to be deluged. Yet, the ego still protectively tries to forestall the inevitable.

Tyrone

I came around the corner, and the door to the bathroom was closed. I thought it was weird because Mishia was at work and the kids were at school. I opened it thinking that maybe the wind had blown it shut or something. The first thing I saw was some juice or something spilled on the white tile. And then I looked closer and I thought, "Hmmm, that looks like blood." I pushed back the shower curtain, and my son was in the bathtub. He had scissors in his left hand, and there were deep cuts on his arms. There was blood everywhere, and his eyes were still open. I felt really calm.

Just as with physical pain, the body often enters a state of shock in order to protect itself from the overwhelming emotional tidal wave that loss presents. Shock serves as a buffer to the pain and defends against the experience of further trauma. It is an adaptive response in that it allows everything to "shut down" while other energies and coping strategies can be mobilized. This experience is often described as a feeling of "numbness" or of being on "autopilot." Thus, a widower may be seen identifying the body of his wife, making funeral arrangements, and coordinating the affairs for incoming guests while appearing quite unaffected. People shake their heads and whisper, "He's doing so well."

Shock and numbness can take on some unlikely faces, such as trying to come outside one's self to avert the intensity of one's pain.

Teresa

My 16-year-old son was having an elective shoulder surgery. I remember hearing the "CODE" while I was in the waiting room. My mother was a nurse and she knew what was going on. She told me that something was happening to Tito. They worked on him for a good 45 minutes, and then the doctor came out to tell me that he was so sorry, there was nothing he could do, that my son was in a coma. I hugged him. And I patted his back and told him that it would all be OK. That afternoon, tons of kids arrived, Tito's friends. I told them all, "Go in there and touch him and tell him that you love him." I was the Mama Bear, taking care of everyone.

Marcia

I saw a military staff car drive by the house, and if you've been in the military, you recognize them right away. Behind that was another car and another car, and I saw them pull into my driveway. And I guess just because of all those years in the military, I clearly knew that something was wrong. I opened the door. There was a chaplain and two other people and a commander who was dressed in an orange and white flight suit. I walked outside and I said, "What's happened?" He said, "Marcia, we need to go inside, there's been an accident"—and so they walked me back inside the house. They said that Steve's plane had crashed and that he was dead. I remember being fairly calm but I was deathly cold. Even now it makes me cold. I called my parents and I said to my mom, "Steve's been killed in a plane crash, you need to come." And she said, "We'll be there right away." Then we went upstairs and I remember . . . this is really bizarre . . . I said, "Would you like some coffee?" Strange. I know, this need to fix coffee for people. So I made some coffee.

By coming outside of themselves and focusing on the needs of others, these women were in a sense, protecting themselves from the pain that they intuitively know will soon inundate them. Suffering triggers a complicated series of reactions, both internally and externally.

One of these reactions is that we may simply refuse to believe that our loved one is gone. We may say to ourselves that this is all a big mistake or a bad dream. Perhaps someone is tricking us. The opportunity for deceit is exacerbated when there is no body or a closed casket. There is something very powerful and undeniable about seeing a body without its soul. At the deepest level, you understand that the person you love is no longer there. Like shock, denial is our psyche's way of preparing us for the descent—buying time.

Eli

My uncle's plane went down about 500 miles north of Hawaii. The first report from the Search and Rescue team members was that they saw a man clinging to the floating wreckage. When they circled back around, he was gone. It is ridiculous to us that he could be there one minute and then not the next. We think he is on some tropical island sipping mai tais with beautiful dancing girls all around him, dodging some problem. He was a Hell's Angel, you know—and some long arm of the law was just busting his chops.

Christina

After my father died, I had to explain to my 4-year-old son that his Pop was in heaven and not coming back. We talked about it on our 200-mile drive to the funeral, and he seemed very sad. It was a closed casket ceremony, and at the service, my son went up to the podium and said that he would miss his Pop Pop's yelling at his soccer games and picking blueberries together every August. There wasn't a dry eye in the room. He cried in the car on the way home and then fell asleep. A couple of months later, I said, "We're going to visit Nanie." He said, "Oh, cool, and I can't wait to see Pop too!" I felt just awful but I explained, "You know son, Pop Pop died." He responded, "OH NO—NOT AGAIN!"

In an innocent state we are often willing to engage, to feel. But as adults it is quite another matter. It gets too close—too strong. We have fallen in that hole before. We must choose what sort of suffering will be let in and under what conditions.

In the Lindworm story, there is no detouring around unpleasantness, and innocence is symbolically sacrificed through the devouring of the first two princesses. It is a setup for the intuitive psyche to access the wisdom necessary to deal with the "monster." The cobbler's daughter visits the wild hag and is armed with some strategies: slips, whips, lye, and milk.

1. Slips

In a mythological sensibility, the slip conceals the divide and protects the eros, or life-generating energy that emanates from there. The slip serves as more than a barrier though, in that it covers a place of divine incubation. When I was a little girl, my grandmother and I used to sit and watch the birds come to her feeder. When some of the females didn't show up for a while she would say, "Oh isn't it wonderful, they are off covering their eggs, very important work." Thus the slips can be seen as providing safety and serving as a veil-like boundary, or covering, marking off the space for soul germination. And as my grandmother says, it is very important work.

In the story, the cobbler's daughter is told to wear 10 slips. When facing the monster of intense loss, it is imperative to externally fortify one's surroundings in order to protect the creative energy, or soul-life. The mourner must bolster up in preparation for the impending stripping down of layers.

There are practical things that one can do for protection. Allowing yourself to receive help is one. Taking long walks is another. Eating good food, sleeping, drinking tea or water instead of alcohol, saying no to things that will overextend you. Some people like to skip rocks or smash tennis balls into a wall. Like the Lindworm taking off his layers, the work of grieving will peel away the skins, or personas, that you have held for yourself. Skin has long been seen as the boundary between self and others. As you are initiated into the dream space of the intense pain and longing of loss, you will find that where you end and the world begins may seem indistinguishable at times. There will be a rawness, a feeling of being exposed. Like the Lindworm, we are standing naked, awaiting transformation. And like the incubating eggs, new senses of self are about to be birthed.

2. Whips

Within the psyche, the fire of anger can be a potent transformative agent. When the cobbler's daughter stands before the basketful of whips and feels their leathery power, we are reminded of how often intense feelings of rage accompany deep loss. Like the cobbler's daughter running through the streets as a madwoman, we shout our indignation to God, we want to sue, we punish ourselves, and sometimes even direct anger toward the person we lost. We roar like a lion, with its noble authority, voicing fierce guardianship of our territory. We have been wronged. Anger can be seen as an external reaction to our internal sense of profound powerlessness.

Anger is the primordial power of the psyche saying, "NO!" One theorist[3] suggests that anger in young children is an adaptive, instinctual response to being separated from a caregiver. It serves to mobilize the person to seek reunion as well as to communicate to the loved one that further separations will not be tolerated. Evolutionarily speaking, anger can be seen as functional. And in some ways, rage can actually serve to empower us. It is a way of saying, "I AM," and an expression of the fact that someone or something has violated our domain. It speaks with sharp, penetrating intensity and is difficult to ignore, making it potentially a very rich source of information. David

---

[3] John Bowlby, "Process of Mourning," *International Journal of Psychoanalysis,* 42 (1961): 317.

Whyte says, "Anger is the purest form of care, the internal living flame of anger always illuminates what we belong to."[4] It is important to remember that anger is a communication from the part of us that is afraid of being alone, afraid of being in danger, and it needs expression and validation. Like the cobbler's daughter, we must be attendant to the feelings and not move to repress our anger or inappropriately express it, or let it devour us. We need to use its energy and see how it has the potential to offer us clarity—to strip down the layers or false realities. In allowing the soul to say "NO," we then set the foundation for the ability to say "YES" later.

Fairy tales traditionally show us many ways of expressing this anger. For instance, there is the hot anger of a fire-breathing dragon and the cold anger of the Ice Queen.[5] Hot anger arrives intensely and unpredictably, like a wildfire. It arises out of a primitive urge for survival (think of an eagle's talons as they penetrate salmon flesh) and the desire for protection. It is sudden to stir, wreaks chaos, then disappears.

Cold anger plays itself out in the interminable grudge, in stewing resentment, and in a vigilant attentiveness to further perceived slights. This anger seems as substantial and immovable as a glacier, and is just as effective in changing the psychological landscape of all those in its path.

Anger is a force that we have been given strange advice about. Girls are taught to be "nice" and are rewarded for repress-

---

[4] David Whyte, Consolations (Langley: Many Rivers Press), 13.
[5] Clarissa Pinkola-Estés, Women Who Run With the Wolves (New York: Ballantine, 1997), 397-401. See this section for a detailed discussion of injured instinct and rage, collective rage, and being stuck in rage.

ing their anger. Boys are shown from an early age that they must demonstrate a reptilian lack of feeling but use their anger to dominate others.[6] In our ill-equipped state, we are often told to "think positive thoughts" and "look on the bright side." This advice can be compared to telling a homeless person to "just buy a house." The toxicity of anger needs special care and containment. We need love and a safe place for catharsis much as a river needs its shores for containment and direction. And when guided attentively, anger is subject to the same rhythms as all natural cycles. It rises, is expressed, begins decaying and then, in death, has it energy redistributed.[7]

The Lindworm story illustrates that the cobbler's daughter is accessing a response that is an integration of the Dragon *and* Ice Queen energies—though there is nothing lukewarm about it. She does not explode in a destructive tirade. Nor does she spend her life seething about her predicament or passively-aggressively torturing her father—or drowning her feelings in excesses or self-damaging activities. She picks up a whip and begins breaking down the monster. In doing so, she accesses the primal life-force energy and gives expression to her outrage in premeditated deliberation. Confidently, the cobbler's daughter channels her anger into creative transformation rather than destruction—a delicate and difficult, albeit essential state to strive for when expressing deep pain.

---

[6] Aaron Kipnis, "Men, Movies, and Monsters: Heroic Masculinity as a Crucible of Male Violence," *Psychological Perspectives: A Quarterly Journal of Jungian Thought, 29, 1* (1994): 38-51.

[7] Pinkola-Estés, 382.

The whips are deliberately used until they are broken and then they are discarded. It is important to note the transience of anger as a defense because it burns our creative energies and eventually leaves us exhausted. Its continued existence (over many years) means that we are being held hostage by Ice Queen energy and have not learned to identify the presence of the shores that will channel our feelings.

3. Wood Ashes and Lye

After the basketful of whips has been spent, the cobbler's daughter confidently picks up the gelatinous blob of the Lindworm and places him in a tub of wood ashes and lye. These agents are ingredients used to make soap. Thus, this moment can be seen as a need for cleansing, or washing away, of old senses of self, as well as a tending of ancient wounds.

Many sacred ceremonies begin with ritual purification. As an example, the Christian baptismal practice enacts the immersion as an initiation. The participant is seen to be drowning a former self and being reborn into a different self that is free of sins and old burdens.

The lye bath may also have disinfectant qualities. Each cut is like a little open mouth with a story to tell: a story of pain, marginalization and shame. Like repressed (monstrous) aspects of the psyche, each wound needs to be tended to, soothed, and washed clean to prevent further festering. Healing can only occur after such loving ablutions.

4. Milk

After the monster is cleansed, the cobbler's daughter lovingly picks him up and places him in a tub of milk. Milk is the ideal food, a reminder of the nurturing mother and the abundance of the earth. It is the original experience of love, belonging, and protection for all mammals.

It is interesting to note that the image of milk does not just refer to the paradisiacal view of the richness of a woman's body. It can also be attributable to descriptions of the fertility of land. An example is the importance of the "promised land" in the Old Testament of the Bible. The original Hebrew is "e-retz za-vat ha-lav oo–d'vash"; translated, *land* (e-retz) *flowing with* (za-vat) *milk* (ha-lav) *and* (oo–) *honey* (d'vash) referenced a place of salvation and goodness. An important link to understanding the word "milk" in this context is an appreciation of its human sexual associations. Variants of the word are used elsewhere in the scriptures to refer to the bodily fluids emanating from the genitals of either a woman or a man. Thus milk can be seen as a germinal, life-generating force that arises out of an integration of masculine and feminine energies.

We see this association in many religions where milk is used as a symbol of mystic rebirth. For instance, the ancient Egyptians practiced a custom of washing the newly deceased in milk to sustain them in rebirth into the next life. In Christianity the communion of the newly baptized included a bath of milk. Thus the Lindworm is being immersed in a life-generating salve, growing into a new wholeness.

With Fate as the guide, death initiates us into a new state of affairs. We must remember that the cobbler's daughter becomes the "Princess" and the chief becomes a "Chief." We may put on the temporary blindfolds of shock and denial. We may become madwomen or madmen. We may be temporarily soothed by the stack of well-meaning "In Sympathy" cards and the casseroles lining the refrigerator shelves. But the call has been trumpeted. It is time to suspend logic and trust our intuitive urges, like Nyctea in the dark, gathering the treasures of the forest. In the Tlingit tale, the chief approaches his "Lindworm" (the terrifying aspects) with a fluid but deliberate series of actions. He seems to know what he needs to do at each juncture, and none of his responses become pathologized, or ill. He wants help and he calls for it. He desires a statue in his wife's likeness and he searches from village to village to find a carver who can craft one. He dresses the statue in the clothes of his deceased wife, and no one questions his sanity. Not a single villager shakes his or her head and tells him that it's time he "move on." His process is quite organic and demonstrates a profound respect for his intuitive inclinations. An extension of this observation is that he moves gracefully in the awareness that we are governed by rhythms that are oftentimes out of our control. Like Nyctea, wildish woman of the forest, he comes to know that life is an interminable series of deaths and rebirths.

Historically, death has been known as a spiritual transformer. In Neolithic times, the deceased were often surrounded by a triangle of cowry shells with traces of red ochre rubbed around the ring. The shell is shaped very much like a pelvis, and the ochre is said to represent birthing blood. It has been speculated that the ancients saw the death in this world as an initiation or birthing into another.[8] It is not just the deceased who are being birthed into a new existence; the bereaved, too, are undergoing an initiation. We are moving from a state of immaturity to a more developed sense of self. And we can assist one another on these parallel journeys.

---

[8] Marija Gimbutas, *The Language of the Goddess* (San Francisco: Harper-Collins, 1991), 100.

"Countless millions crowd the depths of the psyche, waiting for imagination to give them wings." [1]

Greg Mogenson

3

Gathering Bones

After the chief's wife dies, he searches through all the villages in the hope of finding the best woodcarvers to make a statue that is a likeness of his wife. Similarly, Nyctea begins sculpting the bird from her memory, using the gathered bones, feathers, and clay from seasonal riverbeds. They are beginning the search for answers to the questions, "Who was she...*really?*", and, "What was the meaning of her life?", "Where is she?", and "Who will help me through?" It is a desperate time of searching externally in an attempt to concretize the lost person, before he or she slips into the intangible emptiness that death often presents.

"Who were they?" It is important to remember that when loved ones die, we are denied a relationship with the physical person, but we continue to have access to them through our own and others' memories. We look through old pictures and trade stories with others. We vie for their belongings and smell their clothing. We turn toward sources that have provided answers for us in the past and ask them where our loved ones are. We want to know if they are OK. We are trying to carve out a new place for them in the vivid world of our imaginations, and

---

[1] Greg Mogenson, *Greeting the Angels* (New York: Baywood, 1992), xii.

51

in our own idea about the afterlife. Like the chief commissioning his statue and Nyctea re-creating the image of the lost bird, we need something as solid as possible to love because we are not ready to stop loving.

As mourners, we actively gather bits and pieces of the story, searching in the multiple nooks and crannies of our memory banks. It is like participating in a psychological scavenger hunt. This process is an important part of the work of grief because these collective appearances of lost loved ones in thought, conversation, or dreams become the integrated images, or the *angels*, if you will, whose visitations will carry us through.[2] In a sense, it is through physically losing someone that it may be psychologically possible to actually discover them—and ourselves.

This process of mythologizing, or making stories out of the splinters of remembered experience, is one of the ways in which a physical person is transformed into a psychological integrity. Imaginal sights, sounds, and smells all come back through the story we tell ourselves about our loved ones. Uncle Harry liked singing Frank Sinatra in his underwear on Sunday mornings. Father's fingerprints are on every onion-skinned page of that copy of the Bible. Nonie just loved "putting up" those ham pies for Easter. My brother used to say, "Never be the first one to let go in a hug."

A poignant example of story-making in bereavement comes from a frank and heartfelt book called *Beyond Tears: Living After Losing a Child*.[3] In it, nine mothers who have lost their children relay stories and offer suggestions for coping with what most would

---

[2] Mogenson, 13.
[3] Ellen Mitchell, Rita Volpe, Ariella Long, Phyllis Levine, Barbara Goldstein, Barbara Eisenberg, Lorenza Collette, Audrey Cohen, Carol Barkin, *Beyond tears: living after losing a child* (New York: St. Martin's Griffin, 2009).

agree is one of the most difficult losses. Throughout the book, each mother introduces you to her child. Jessie planted kernels of popcorn to see if they would grow and taught her dog how to "communicate" by tickling his chin and getting him to nod. Marc had a wonderful sense of humor, sporting a "My parents just think I went to college" T-shirt under his graduation robe. Andrea was a cheerful socialite who could often be seen talking on two phones at once. These are the details, the colors, the textures, the sounds that come together to help you discover your loved ones. It is an important task to reconstruct them because the story becomes an invisible lifeline through which we still connect and *still love*.

Our psyches may also try to piece together and connect with the deceased during this early phase through identifying[4] with the lost loved one. That is, we may take on characteristics of the dead in an attempt to revivify those aspects of the deceased that are now beyond reach. We may listen to their music, wear their clothes, eat their favorite foods, or find ourselves spouting their life philosophies.

Ms. Francis

I spend a great deal of time each week ironing my clothes. As the Vice President of my corporation, and the only woman

---

[4] For a more extensive, academic discussion of identification, see Otto Fenichel, *The Psychoanalytic Theory of Neurosis,* (New York: Norton, 1945), 395; Erik Lindemann, "Symptomology and Management of Acute Grief," *American Journal of Psychiatry,* 101 (1944): 142; George Pollock, "Mourning and Adaptation," *International Journal of Psychoanalysis,* 42 (1961): 354; Lorraine D. Siggins, "Mourning: A Critical Survey of the Literature," *International Journal of Psychoanalysis* (1966): 47.

in upper management, it is important that I present well, conduct myself with discipline, and command respect. After my 21-year-old, liberally minded son died in car accident, I found myself in an unusual circumstance. I was in the front row of a Phish concert in a tie-dyed T-shirt—and I felt the urge to "spin." As I collapsed in laughter and my tie-dyed skirt rode up, I looked down and realized that I hadn't shaved my legs in over three months. I knew my son was watching me and was very pleased.

Jacob

I am the oldest of three children. When I was 15, my sister Lila died in a waterskiing accident. She was only 12. Lila was always the funny one in our family. She used to ask my mom to drive through the roundabout over and over because it made her laugh so much to be breaking the rules. And my mom would do it, because everyone laughed when Lila was laughing. It was hard not to. At our family dinner parties, if the adults were laughing louder at another table, she would tell all the kids at our table to laugh even louder, to make it look like we were having a better time. I used to do this belly laugh, and my stomach would hurt after a while, but I was having such a good time. We all were. After Lila died, our family became so serious. Everyone was so sad all the time. And even though I was the serious one before, I found myself trying to be funny. I'm not as good as Lila at being funny, but when I make someone laugh, I think of Lila and how she would like that. When I got my driver's license, I would sometimes drive around the roundabout three whole times, just because.

The desire to identify with the dead can also play itself out in our bodies. Our heads hurt. Our stomachs wrench. Our hearts ache. We can't breathe. Grief can be amazingly physical. Our bodies are communicating with us about the unspeakable and showing us the specific textures of our loss when it is difficult to do so consciously. It is important to acknowledge what the body is saying, to notice and to name it. It is one way of more fully integrating the experience and understanding its complexities.

Tara

After my brother's death, I remember walking through the grocery store feeling as if my legs weren't attached to my body. While I was negotiating the syrupy haze, it was hard to believe that other people could just continue on as normal, as if nothing had happened.

Alexa

My husband died of a sudden heart attack at age 40. The really hard part is that it was on the third day of a trial separation, and I felt as if I had literally broken his heart, that it was all my fault. Soon after, I found myself at the emergency room because I thought I was having a heart attack. After the EKG revealed no abnormalities, I told them, "Something is *really* wrong, I just know it." The doctors nodded condescendingly and gave me a referral for counseling. But I kept trying to tell them, "My heart is literally broken."

Juan

My friend Charlie and I were riding on the back of a hydro-seeding truck on a job near Sacramento. We were facing each other and we were laughing. Charlie was about six inches closer to the front of the truck and turned to look as the driver went through a low underpass. I watched his head smack on the concrete, and he was knocked over. We took Charlie to the ER, but the swelling in his brain was too much for his skull to take. He looked like the Elephant Man and it was hard to even recognize him as human. They pulled the plug two days after the accident. I had a throbbing, intense headache in my forehead for about two months after Charlie's death. Nothing I did would help, it was so bad.

Lauren

I had been having an affair with Richard for a year when it happened, and we were closer than ever at that time. He was vacationing with his wife and children in Hawaii, and he was hit by a big wave and just never came up. It was true hell for me, because he just stopped returning my text messages and I found out in the newspaper. I couldn't go to the funeral, and I couldn't tell anyone except my closest friend about how I was feeling. She wasn't terribly sympathetic because she had lots of judgment about our relationship. I was a mess, and yet I had no place in Richard's "legit" life, and as "illegit" as my pain may have been, it was real to me. As I read the article in the paper, my chest became extremely tight. To this day, every time I think of Richard, I cannot breathe. I literally cannot breathe and feel as if I am going to die, too. Sometimes I wish I just would.

Another way in which we try to concretize our lost loved ones is by offering our physical bodies as hosts for them. An anthropologist in the 1950s[5] noticed that in certain New Guinea tribes, it was common for the mourners to eat a piece of the flesh of the corpse to incorporate the dead person's personality into the living. This practice may have been a ritual enactment of what psychologists call *introjection*.[6] The idea is that one's beloved is not actually gone but continues to live on in you. Lola's story is a particularly poignant example.

Lola

Papa was meaner and madder than a swarm of wasps, especially after he'd had a few Jacks. It was pretty common for him to leave me alone with my baby sister when he'd be down to the

---

[5] Peter Marris, *Widows and Their Families* (London: Routledge & Kegan Paul, 1954), 31.

[6] For a more extensive, academic discussion of introjection see Karl Abraham, *Selected Papers on Psychoanalysis* (London: Hogarth, 1924/1949), 435-436; Otto Fenichel, *The Psychoanalytic Theory of Neurosis* (New York: Norton, 1945), 394; Sigmund Freud, "Mourning and Melancholia," in *Collected Works, Vol. 4,* ed. J. Riviere (New York: Basic, 1917/1959), 154; George Pollock, "Mourning and Adaptation," *International Journal of Psychoanalysis,* 42 (1961): 350; Marris, 31; Roy Schafer, *Aspects of Internalization* (New York: Philosophical, 1968), 138.

Paddle Wheel. He'd put a plastic snake on the threshold of the door and tell me that if I walked out for any reason, that snake would come to life and bite me, and then I'd have to go be with Mama in the ground. I was only 5 years old. One night, when he'd been gone a long time, I put the baby to sleep in the drawer in my bedroom. I heard him come in and the bottles on the counter hit the floor. I knew to lie real still. Sometimes if I was asleep and good, he wouldn't bother me. I squeezed my eyes shut and didn't move. The door kind of opened sideways because one of the hinges had come loose, and I could hear him taking his belt off. That wasn't a good thing, when Papa took his belt off. And then Lisa began crying. It was weird because she was doing what I was thinking and I almost wondered if it was me or her making the noise. So I clamped my mouth shut and tried not to even breathe. But the sound kept happening—kind of a low whimpering. Papa began yelling, and when I opened my eyes, I could see the spittle coming out of his mouth with the light coming in from the window. He was mad and he picked up a pillow and put it over Lisa's face. He just held it there—pushing—until she didn't cry anymore. And this moment is clear as day—because a white wisp of angel light sat up out of Lisa's body and kind of looked around. Papa stood up and walked out of the room quietly. And this angel light, it floated across the room and came and wrapped itself all around me. But then I could feel it inside me. It was all warm. And I knew right there that Lisa was going to stay with me and that I had to take care of her.

This response was a soul-saving one. Lola kept Lisa alive by incorporating her into her own body and allowed them both to survive, for the short term. When I met Lola, she was 38 years old and struggling with carrying Lisa within her. She remarked that even the simplest decisions were very conflicted. Lola wanted to live in Hawaii, and Lisa wanted to stay in Nevada and attend school. Lola became attracted to men that Lisa despised. Lisa had even become a vegan for a while, much to the dismay of her host. After much time and attentiveness, it became clear that she could integrate aspects of Lisa (like her desire to make healthy decisions) that she enjoyed and allow the other parts to "pass on." When the time felt right, we did a guided meditation where she allowed that "wisp of angel light" to leave her body and go toward the light. She was assured that she had done a beautiful job of caring for her sister, but that moving on would benefit her and her sister. Lola sobbed and expressed her deep relief. She said she felt free.

Later that year, Lola gave birth to a baby who would only live for a few hours—her only attempt at biological motherhood. The hospital allowed her to take her daughter, whom she named "Alisa," with her so that she could die at home. I sat with Lola while she rhythmically moved in a rocking chair, holding her dying child. I was so worried that she wouldn't be able to sustain another tragic loss. She was singing a made-up song that sounded so much like a young child's. The words were "Angel light in heaven....sister love.....sister love....take our baby... into you ...sister love, sister love..." And her daughter died. And she rocked and rocked, for two more days. And then she buried her.

It could be argued that Lola needed to fully incorporate both Lisas, or imprint them permanently in her imagination, before being able to let them go. And again, "letting go" doesn't mean that loving stops. It means that a transformation is allowed in the relationship.

When Nyctea assembles the talons, feathers, and bones, and when the Chief commissions artists to make a woodcarving of his wife, they are each resurrecting the dead by piecing the lost one back together. We need to move them from the abstract back to the concrete. It is out of this desire to re-create the image of the deceased and sustain connection that people may do some seemingly peculiar things. A 9/11 widow confesses on national TV that she spent all of the money that had been given to her through donations and insurance to help her raise her sons on a collection of expensive shoes. She said her husband loved when she wore sexy shoes. A mother who lost her son in Iraq is nearly arrested for sleeping on top of the Tomb of the Unknown Soldier. On what would be her wedding day, a bereaved woman invites her friends and family to the church and walks down the aisle alone dressed in black lace, holding a bouquet of black roses. One couple took their son's ashes on every road trip they endeavored, so as not to leave him alone. They strapped the box into a seat belt in the back seat. Grief is as unique as our own relationship with the deceased and can be a very creative process. It can be surprising how it manifests—in both ourselves and others.

The re-creation of the image of the deceased is something most of us do very unconsciously, through identification, introjection, and storytelling. This mythologizing, or piecing together of memories, pictures, objects, among other things, is one of the ways in which the evaporated person takes form again. According to Jung, these integrities cannot be reduced to memories. They are "a concept derived from poetic usage, namely a figure of fancy or fantasy-image, which is related indirectly to the perception of an external object."[7] In this view, the deceased are images through which the imagination can continue to be alive, despite the fact that the physical body has been lost. Though the dead lose their material reality, they are thought to gain a psychological one, changed by death. This psychic reality is as much a product of the bereaved's unconscious as it is a representation of the deceased person, invested in both personal and consensual power. Thus the integrity is created out of that which lies *between* the living and the dead, and those dynamics supply the metaphors upon which symbols of the dead can be modeled (see Chapter 5).

Another important question to ask during this early part of grief work is, "Where are they?" Part of authoring our loved one's stories, and our own in relation to them, is familiarizing ourselves with our own beliefs about the afterlife.[8] For Lola, her Lisas were in heaven. A Jewish man explained that his deceased mother went to "sheoul," or the dark realm of departed spirits. Teresa's Tito is with her Grandma Marin. Among the Inuits, their dead are dancing in the northern lights. Some believe that spiritual energy has rejoined the energy of the natural world.

---

[7] Carl Jung in eds. Carrie Rothgeb & Siegfried Clemens, *Abstracts of the Collected Works of C.G. Jung* (Princeton: Princeton University Press, 1992), 442.
[8] Notable books on worldwide beliefs about life after death. For a spectrum of religious beliefs: Frnaz Ma'Sumian, *Life After Death: A Study of the Afterlife in World Religions* (Oxford: Oneworld. 1995); For more of an emphasis on cultural beliefs: Brian Innes, *Death and the Afterlife* (New York: St. Martin's, 1999); Colin Parkes, Pittu Laungani, and William Young, eds., *Death and Bereavement Across Cultures* (New York: Routledge, 1997). And for those who are interested in visionary encounters with the deceased: Raymond Moody, *Life After Life* (New York: Harper Collins, 1975/2015).

In figuring out what we believe, we are helping not only ourselves, but our loved ones in that we are actively creating a place for them.

Some of us have a more difficult time placing our loved ones in some place beyond because we haven't thought about it or nothing in particular resonates with us.

Seana

After my brother died, my 3-year-old son asked me, "What happens to you when you die? Where is Jim?" I saw this as an opportunity to introduce him to the religious traditions of the world. "Well the Buddhists believe...and the Catholics believe...and some Native Americans believe..." Frustrated, he said, "Yes, yes, Mommy, but what do *we* believe?" Indeed.

Some may remember the story of Sarah Bernhardt, a French actress who performed around the turn of the century (1900). She was booked in all the major cities across the U.S., and her shows were sold out. Eager New Yorkers crowded the theater and watched dumbstruck as Sarah serenaded them in French. An urgent message was sent back to her producers in France, "SEND THE TRANSLATION." When the librettos arrived, someone realized that they were the translations for the wrong show. Giving in to the audience's demands for an explanation of what they were seeing, the theater employees distributed them anyway. Thousands of people thumbed through their librettos, trying to match the written words on the page to the performance they were witnessing onstage. And for the most part, they were delighted. Each person applied the template to whatever part of her show fit his or her understanding of it—which might be a lovely metaphor for negotiating through life.

Which libretto, or belief system, have you been using to gain an understanding of what happened to your loved one? How well does it fit your experience of this loss? Is there such a thing as a true libretto? Reacquainting yourself and/or exploring your own and others' belief systems is an important task in beginning to feed the starving soul. It is a period of situating one's own pain and ascertaining its meaning—seeing its rhythms and seeking out others who have navigated through similar patterns. One story that speaks to these rhythms is an old European folktale called "Godfather Death." This story presents many universal images, and it reflects a great number of worldwide beliefs about the nature of death. It is offered here as an example of one "libretto," or way of understanding and situating the intense experience of loss.

Godfather Death

A long time ago, in a village with twisted lanes, there was a peasant who had twelve children. He was so poor that he boiled the hides of his dead animals to make a glue-like mash to feed his children, and he sent them digging through refuse piles to find scraps of discarded food. This man was already indebted to his family, friends, and neighbors. So, when the thirteenth child came into the world, he had nowhere to turn to find a godfather for his son and he decided to go into the lanes and ask the first person he came across.

The first person who came his way was a luminous being in a shining, white cloak. With a glow that sent diamond glints into the air, the being said, "I am God, and I know what is in your heart. I will be the godfather of your son." The man hesitated for a moment looking this way and that and mostly at the ground, and replied, "I thank you kindly, but I am going to say no. You see, you give to the rich and let the poor starve and you are not a fair man. I'll be going on my way, now." And he smiled and bowed, and went on his way.

Around the next corner, the man saw a being in a red cloak, with fiery eyes like glowing embers. With a spew of sparks, the being said, "I am the Devil, and I know what's in your heart, I will be the Godfather of your son." The man hesitated for a moment looking this way and that and mostly at the ground, and replied, "I thank you kindly, but I am going to say no. You see, you prey on the morally weak and avoid the virtuous and you are not a fair man. I'll be going on my way, now." And he smiled and bowed and went on his way.

Around the next corner, the man saw a being in a black cloak, with coal dark eyes and hands like burned branches. With a cloudy breath of dread, the being said, "I am Death, and I know what's in your heart. I will be the Godfather of your son." The man hesitated for a moment looking this way and that and mostly at the ground, and replied, "You take away the rich as well as the poor, without distinction. You are a fair man and shall be my child's godfather."

Death said, "I will make your son the greatest healer in all the land."

The man bowed and smiled and said, "Next Sunday is the baptism." Death came to the baptism, did his part, and then retreated from the boy's life for quite some time.

The thirteenth child had a difficult life. He survived by piecing together bits of clothing and foraging in the forest, sometimes stealing eggs from the neighbor's chickens. One day, when he had come of age, Godfather Death beckoned from behind a tree and re-introduced himself. He took him deep into the woods and showed him an herb that grew there, saying, "Now you shall receive your godfather's present. I will turn you into a famous physician. Whenever you are called to a sick person I will appear to you. If I stand at the sick person's head, you may say with confidence that you can make him well again; then give him some of this herb, and he will recover. But if I stand at the sick person's feet, he is mine, and you must say that he is beyond help, and that no physician in the world could save him."

It was not long before the young man had become the most famous physician in the whole world. People said of him, "He only needs to look at the sick in order to immediately know their condition, whether they will regain their health, or are doomed to die." And people came to him from far and wide, taking him to their sick, and giving him so much money that he soon became a wealthy man.

Now it came to pass that the king became ill. The Physician was summoned and was told to say if a recovery were possible. However, when he approached the bed, Death was standing at the sick man's feet, and so no herb on earth would be able to help him. "If I could only deceive death for once," thought the Physician. "He will be angry, of course, but because I am his godson he will shut one eye. I will risk it." He therefore took hold of the sick man and laid him the other way around, so that Death was now standing at his head. Then he gave the king some of the herb, and he recovered. But when the physician left the room, Death was standing outside the door. Death held him firmly by the arm, and said, "You cannot interfere with my work. It is not for you to decide who lives and who dies, do you understand me?" The physician apologized and assured Death that it would never happen again.

Soon afterward the king's daughter became seriously ill. She was his only child, and he cried day and night until his eyes were going blind. Then he proclaimed that whosoever rescued her from death should become her husband and inherit the crown. When the physician came to the sick girl's bed he saw Death at her feet. He should have remembered his promise to his Godfather, but he was so infatuated by the princess's great beauty and the prospect of becoming her husband that he threw all thought to the winds. He quickly lifted up the sick girl and placed her head where her feet had been. Then he gave her some of the herb, and her cheeks immediately turned red, and life stirred in her once again. This time, Death did not wait for the Physician to leave the room, but came by his side and ushered him out and down the hallway with his ice-cold hand. Death said, "I want to show you something." And they descended a dank, stony stairwell that went down and down and down, towards an underground cavern. There the Physician saw thousands and thousands of candles were burning in endless rows, some large, others medium-sized, others small. Every instant some died out, and others were relit, so that the little flames seemed to be jumping about in constant change.

"See," said Death, "These are the life-lights of all creatures."

The Physician said, "Well, these are very nice, indeed, but I need to return to the castle and marry my bride. I have a kingdom to rule over and I should be getting back, if you'll just excuse me."

Death held fast to his arm and asked if the Physician would like to see his candle. The Physician nervously said, "Well no, not really, I mean all the big ones are for little children and the little ones are for old people who have lived a long life, yes?"

Death shook his head somberly from side to side and explained, "No, some of the little, sputtering candles are for children and some of the big thick ones are for adults. Now, don't you want to see your own life-light?"

Finally understanding Death's meaning, and thinking that it still would be very large, the Physician said, "Very well, then, let me see."

Death pointed to a little stump that was just threatening to go out, and said, "See, there it is."

"Oh, dear Godfather," said the horrified Physician, "Light a new one for me. Do it as a favor to me, so that I can enjoy my life, and become king and the husband of the beautiful princess."

"I cannot," answered Death, "one must go out before a new one is lighted."

"Then set the old one onto a new one that will go on burning after the old one is finished," begged the physician." Death took hold of a large new candle and set it on top of the little one, extinguishing the flame. The physician immediately fell to the ground, and he too was now in the hands of Death.

·◆·

In depth psychology,[9] the appearance of the three figures in their colored cloaks is symbolically significant. Black, White, and Red grouped together often represent the alchemical stages of transformation. Alchemy is the ancient practice of turning base materials into precious metals like gold, but has been adapted to metaphorically refer to the processes employed by people to individuate, or develop psychologically. Black (nigredo) often refers to the eclipse of familiar patterns of identity and meaning, the death of reason, disintegration, and the shadow. This energy represents the unconscious "dark" part of the psyche, such as unlived possibilities and the propensity for evil. It is seen as one stage in the three-part development. If this stage is successfully negotiated, meaning that one is able to face the darkest feelings in oneself and integrate them or sit in the abyss and fully experience them, without moving to hide or repress the uncomfortable feelings, the next phase is the White (albedo). White is a state of newness and beginning, illumination, or something coming into conscious awareness. Consider white apple, pear, and orange blossoms as a sign of spring and renewal. If these contradictory energies of dark and light are held in tension and attended to, then Red (rubedo) follows. Red is a symbol of life and creation. One example of this energy is the redness of blood. There is the regenerative blood of menstruation or childbirth, which signifies a new beginning. Conversely, there is the blood that leaves the body during

---

[9] Depth Psychology is composed of approaches that give credence to the presence of the unconscious. Some of these are: Psychoanalytic, Jungian, and Archetypal Psychologies.

woundedness and portends death. Another red symbol is fire, which warms and protects, but is also capable of catastrophic destruction. Red is the binding of opposites and the subsequent formation of new possibilities. These three phases, in any individual's psychological work, repeat themselves endlessly, with a pattern of darkness, light, holding and release of energy. In "Godfather Death," these themes appear not only in the colors of the cloaks, but in the symbol of the candles. A candle is lit, a candle is doused, and there is a release or change of energy. The old life (or ways of being) must be extinguished before a new one can be born. According to the story, when it is your time, it is your time. There is no negotiating with Fate. The task is not only to surrender to the larger force of Death, but also to know that a new candle cannot be lit until the old candle is doused.

This rhythm is natural, as Godfather Death points out when he mentions that the Physician must not interfere with his work. But as humans, we are often like the Physician, and we feel a need to manipulate Death and control its circumstances. It can be healthy to be proactive in the face of death and to take all measures possible to keep the flame burning of ones we love. However, bereaved people are often plagued with guilt and ruminate about the decisions they made after a loved one is gone. "If only I had…." Or, "I should have been able to stop it." If it was a long illness, we often become confused about the treatment strategies that were chosen. Were they too much, or perhaps not enough? Is there something we didn't think of? In our culture, control is considered a condition of well-being, and it is very hard for us to concede that there are things outside of our influence.

Jorge

My wife, she had a bad stomach, and we brought her to the doctor. She said that Alejandra was very stressed and should learn how to meditate, and exercise more. For two months, my Alejandra sat and tried to do nothing for 10 minutes a day and walked around our block, and still her pain was bad. One night she was feeling real bad, and we went to the emergency room. They told us that she was starting her time of menopause and that this was cramps. But she was in so much pain, moaning every night. Two months later, we went to another doctor, who finally ordered a test, and they found things inside of her. They said they were fibroids and nothing to worry about. She had to have an operation to take all of it out, and they told us the next week that they were cancer. They told us not to worry again because they got all of it. Two months later the cancer was in her lungs. My Alejandra, such a beautiful woman, had to take these medicines that make her sick and lose all of her hair. The food taste no good to her no more. I am angry for her pain. So angry. Now I just cry and cry and cry to think of what I should have done. I should have done something. I should not have believed them. I should have taken better care of her, and it is all my fault. My poor Alejandra who is with God.

Metta

When I went into early labor, I thought, "This can't be happening to me....it's TOO SOON." My son had different ideas

and was born weighing 1 pound 7 ounces. He was barely clinging to life, a repetition of spikes on a monitor. His perfect little
hands didn't squeeze your finger, and his eyes really didn't see,
but his heart was beating. It seemed to be saying, "I am here. I
am here." My husband cried when he saw him, saying over and
over "our son....our son..." and our love was immediate and
profound. If we could will him to live, we would have, but instead we consented, enthusiastically, to a chaos of medical in-
terventions. We wanted him so badly. Tubes came out of his
translucent hand, stomach, and mouth, and wires were pasted
all over his little chest. Each day was a roller coaster of hope and
despair with multiple surgeries to fix the hole in his heart, the
bleeding in his brain. He was wracked with antibiotics after bat-
tles with infection. And still we hoped. Our lives were a barrage
of statistics, chances of cerebral palsy, cognitive impairment,
blindness, deafness. Still, we loved. Still, his heart said, "I am
here." Still we subjected this little angel to an unspeakable number of medical agonies.

After three months and two days, he just gave out. It was like
being kicked into a long plateau of anguish, as the line on the
monitor just continued to be flat. As I held his tiny body, so
fragile and so beaten, I tried to draw him into myself, to hold
him inside of me. And then it hit me. "We did this to him. We
made his short time on earth a living hell." I don't know if I can
ever forgive myself. I really don't know.

⸱⸱❖⸱⸱

It is human to review our actions, to ask the question, "Why
didn't I?", or to be plagued with anger at God, ourselves, or those
we hold responsible. It may serve to better direct decisions in

the future. However, "Godfather Death" shows that getting stuck in trying to manipulate death is like being the Physician. Switching up fate is a strategy that only works in the short term, and eventually, there are forces much larger than an individual will or modern medicine that determine how and when someone dies. It is the ego that produces guilt (I could have controlled this!) and serves to erode self-worth, which leaves some bitter and humiliated. These emotions, though understandable, add layers of obstruction to being able to sit in a place of love for our lost ones and in compassion for ourselves. Gathering bones, or actively making loved ones into imaginal integrities, understanding ourselves in relation to them, and situating these experiences can help one move from humiliation to simply humility. It is an active process that allows the bereaved to engage again.

When "gathering bones," we are being asked to sort through and identify the beliefs and behaviors that will sustain us and separate those from the ones that will not. This mythic theme has been presented in many familiar stories. The Grimms' version of Cinderella has her sorting lentils and peas (nourishment) from the ashes (dead energy) in the fireplace. The Russian Vasalisa must separate a mountain of poppy seeds (painlessness, sleep, or death) from dirt (fertility), and a pile of mildewed corn (poison) from good corn (sustenance). And the Greek Psyche must sift through a mingled pile of wheat, barley, millet, poppy seed, peas, lentils, and beans to appease her angry mother-in-law, Aphrodite. Sorting, showing discrimination, knowing what is good for you and what is bad is a fundamental task for any person, but especially for those who are in deep pain.

According to myths and folktales throughout the world, we are not alone in trying to exercise this discrimination. Joseph Campbell said, "One has only to know and trust, and the ageless guardians will appear. Having responded to his own call, and continuing to follow courageously as the consequences unfold, the hero finds all the forces of the unconscious at his side. Mother Nature herself supports the mighty task."[10] These ageless guardians often assist by offering amulets (protective charms) or animal guides. Cinderella's bird friend appears to assist her. Vasalisa is aided by a little doll that had been given to her by her dying mother. In Psyche's task, an army of ants comes to her support. Even in more modern stories, we see Harry Potter receiving an invisibility cloak. Or Neo, in *The Matrix*, having a team of computer scientists who can download jujitsu programs at will.

Leo

When I first entered the terrifying space of loss, I didn't know who my guides were. My own search to situate my brother in an afterworld ranged from reading ancient religious texts to skeptically looking through books on channeling. I once went to a Life After Life workshop, trying to summon the face of my brother in a mirror. I talked to a psychic and went to a Catholic Mass for the Dead. I climbed Mount Tallac and waited

---

[10] Joseph Campbell, *The Hero with a Thousamd Faces* (Princeton: Princeton University Press, 1973), 72.

for divine wisdom, and later drank a whole six-pack of beer and a bottle of red wine. I think I received divine wisdom, but unfortunately I don't remember it.

Some people intuitively know whom they need, and for others it may take longer to have a sense of the right guide. Choosing a midwife (or husband) to help you usher all the undeveloped images or stories about the deceased into a coherent story is a very important task.

After Teresa returned from the hospital after the death of her son, the first thing she said was, "Find me another mother who has gone through this, I need another mother." Similarly, Anita knew that there were those she could connect to and those she couldn't. Her son's car broke down at a baseball game and the tow truck driver set him up to have his car stolen by leaving him at a remote location. The thieves beat him to the point of unconsciousness and left his body behind a gas station, where he was found two days later, dead from his wounds. This situation was popularized in the news media and referred to as the "9-1-1- Murder Trial," Anita's son, Scott had telephoned 9-1-1 during the incident, and the call had been mis-classified as a lower level of urgence. It was a parent's worst nightmare. In chaos, Anita sought psychotherapeutic treatment. She said, "The first therapist I was referred to was a man in his 30s, who spent the entire 50 minutes writing down everything I said on a yellow pad. He barely looked at me, and I could tell he was uncomfortable. I knew that this man couldn't help me." Anita did connect with a psychologist who had also experienced the loss of her own child. Having someone who could mirror and validate the complexity of her feelings and thoughts was very valuable. In addition to having uptake for her experiences, Anita was eventually able to write a book about her loss and the state of morality in America, which was also cathartic.[11]

We must remember that our deep pain often brings up fear of loss of control and resistance in others. Like us, they have been conditioned to avoid depression, despair, boredom, restlessness, insecurity, and pain, in short—anything unpleasant. It gets too close. It can be too much. The grieving person can represent their worst fear. It is telling that 45 million Americans take some form of antidepressant every day, so it's no wonder that it is very difficult for most people to have authentic, open, feeling responses to loss. People's discomfort can be recognized in many different guises as some choose to launch into hyperactive caretaking, line the refrigerator with food that you will never eat, or offer platitudes, only to disappear when you really need them. In grief workshops participants have shared well-meaning but unhelpful things that people have said to them. You may recognize some of these: "Well you're young, you can always have another child (or another husband/wife)," or "I know exactly how you feel, my horse (or dog or cat or lizard) died when I was 10," or "Aren't you over this yet?" Others on this list are "Time heals," and "At least he's in a better place," or "Look on the bright side, at least you had her for # years." One mother who had lost her child to a brain tumor at age two said that it really bothers her when people say, "After what happened to you, I go home and hug my own child so much tighter." For her, it was a version of "Too bad you don't have a child anymore, but I do," and a reminder of the unfairness

---

[11] Anita Spencer, A Crisis of Spirit: Our Desperate Search for Integrity (Oklahoma City, OK: Insight Books, 1996).

of it all. Another common response is "Everything happens for a reason," or "I guess it was meant to be." These statements, though well-intentioned, are rarely comforting. It is one form of rationalizing the experience (jumping into your head) rather than sitting with the complexity of the feelings and acknowledging them. There can also be a long line of unsolicited advice and "should" statements as well. "You SHOULD...get a job, or volunteer, or get a pet or go to church or start dating again soon." In the Tlingit tale, the Chief needs to find someone in his own village, someone who has seen his relationship, someone who can really help him understand who his wife was and who he is in relation to her. Like Nyctea, who must "know" the bird she is reconstructing, we need to be with people who can really attend to us and help us articulate the particular soulfulness of our beloved. Psychologically, this "someone" is a person who understands the unique complexity of the dynamics of the relationship in life, and in death. They can assist in answering the questions, "Who was your loved one for you?" "Who were you for them?" You and your witness, whether it be a friend, spiritual person, or a therapist, are the archeologists of the psyche. You are conducting your own, private Dia de los Muertos (Day of the Dead) with the artifacts that you gather. In Mexico, the Day of the Dead is a festive occasion, when relatives and friends have a picnic on the grave of the deceased. You and your witness can enact this ritual by sharing pictures, memories, and sacred objects. In hosting the ghosts, you are inviting the abstract back into the concrete. And the stories that are made and shared about this transition become the placenta-like energy that provides nourishment and connection. And it is needed in order to heed the call and make meaning out of our own and our loved ones' lives.

"Each morning, your death
Hangs like weights
On the ends of my lips
Leaving just enough space for gray moans to slip out
And drop all around me."[1]

Estelle Padawer

4

The Abyss

The chief dressed the statue in his dead wife's robe, and the people from his village were astounded at the likeness. He had commissioned an accurate representation of his wife and brought it into his home. In her redwood burl, Nyctea reconstructed from memory an image of the owl complete with feathers and claws, and wide yellow/green eyes. In psychological terms this means that the chief and Nyctea have engaged in the ongoing authoring of the story, and their own, in relation to that which has been lost in this world. At this point, the chief in particular is trying to hold on to his wife, historically. He is, in a sense, saying that he doesn't want to move from who he was, either. This period is a classic juncture in bereavement, in that we desperately cling to whom we need the deceased to be for us, but we are faced with the growing awareness that this old relationship is no longer possible. In a way it is an annihilation

---

[1] Estelle Padawer, "Dirge," in *Inside Grief*, ed. Line Wise (Incline Village: Wise Press, 2001), 31. Reprinted by permission from Wise Press.

of the self, because we don't know who we are separate from our loving. It is also the death of our egos, in that we realize that we are completely powerless. The awareness that we have lost not only our loved one, but our own sense of self, can result in intense pain. We *miss* them. We *need* them. Our suffering requires an agonizing attentiveness. We are forced into an awareness of ourselves, an exposure of the innermost topography of the vulnerabilities that now define who we are. And it is hard to sit with the ugly sides of ourselves.

During this juncture, our psyches often step in and protect us by shutting down. This state is undoubtedly the most utterly desolate and difficult part of grieving. It has been termed *depression, despair*, and *disorganization* by psychologists and *The Abyss*[2] by philosophers, poets, artists, and writers. Physicists and astronomers call it the *black hole*. Its onset marks a shift from looking to externals to fill the void to a turning inward. You are now *in* the void. It is like being trapped in the labyrinth of your own psyche with the realization that the work to follow will be your own, and only your own, and yet you have no energy or inclination to even try it. You have stopped singing, ceased cooking, put away your tools or crafts. You cannot write a word. There is no pleasure. You cannot remember the last time you laughed. It is like being as dried up as the bones themselves.

In a culture that values sunny dispositions, perpetual productivity, and absolute control you may feel yourself a psychological leper. You may hear things like, "Isn't it time that you moved on?" or "Aren't you over that *yet?*" Or the more subtle, but equally dismissive, "Don't you think you should get some help?" This can

---

[2] For an in-depth description of "The Abyss" see Linda Leonard, *Witness to the Fire: Creativity and Veil of Addiction* (Boston: Shambala, 1989), 213-226.

be said lovingly as well, but oftentimes it is not. There is a moment in the original Grimm's version of "Cinderella" when the stepmother instructs one daughter to cut off her toes so that she can fit into the desired slipper and be seen as the true match for the Prince. She does so and is discovered by the birds, who call out, "There's blood within the shoe!" The stepmother then tells the other daughter to cut off her heel to fit into the shoe. She is once again discovered as blood leaks out. Feeling people, like disenfranchised stepsisters, are often asked by the culture to amputate important parts of who they are in order to fit in. People become uncomfortable when "There's blood within the shoe!" But there is, and the shoe doesn't fit. You can't act normal because you don't feel normal. And everyone wants so badly for you to be OK, because it is uncomfortable if you are not, which creates so much pressure. Hiding profound wounding often takes even more energy than feeling profound wounding. The natural response to the overwhelming pain and attempts to mask it is to withdraw. You have been in a chronic state of emotional overload and physical stress, so it is no wonder that the body says, *shut down and conserve*. Like the turtle, who retreats into its shell, the bereaved need to be shielded from the elements of the external world. Even with this protection, it still feels like dark chaos. It is here that one is required to sit with helplessness, fear, depression, loneliness, boredom, pain, impotence, confusion and discomfort—extreme discomfort.

Marcia

After my husband died in an airplane accident, it was like I was in a hole and I kept trying to crawl out of it, and someone else would come along and throw some more dirt on top of me. I couldn't catch my breath, just more and more dirt. Dirt in my eyes so I couldn't see, in my hair, under my fingernails, so I couldn't feel. Dirt between my legs and under my arms. Dirt in my ears so I could no longer hear. Dirt gagged me, my mouth was filled with its taste. It piled higher and higher and got so heavy. I didn't want to shower because I deserved this feeling. I could not sleep and I had a hard time eating anything. I dropped down to 89 pounds, became amenorrheal and didn't care whether I lived or died. I was dead, really, a little feather of a nonperson under all that dirt. Living hell.

Walt

It's been 10 years, but if someone says my son's name, I fall into that pit. I try to wave my arms backward, but I am always standing at the edge, and the slightest memory of him puts me off balance. My chest begins to burn, and my tongue gets sticky, and then I have that distinct sensation of FALLING. And it's all dark.

Nora

My 16-year-old son died in a car accident. His friend's car skidded out of control and it slid to a stop, upside down in the Truckee River. One month later, my husband died of a sudden heart attack. The two people whom I most wanted to touch, to smell, to feel, to know myself through had evaporated. I lay on my bed, thinking of both of their bodies next to me, but my arms ache with emptiness. There is air, black space, void upon void upon void.

Liz Crow, in her poem "A Certain Knowing," communicated it well: "So this is grief. When hearts wrench and senses numb. Tears make salt-water truth. And in the long spaces, birdsong cheats the silence and affronts the soul."[3]

It is during this period of pain, and subsequent withdrawal and conservation, that something important is happening. It may be hard to recognize or name it because it is difficult to feel anything but hopelessness; but the soul is at work, remaking the sense of self, and offering a movement to humility, and maybe even opportunities for connection.

Though pain is extremely uncomfortable, it can also offer some silver linings. When in pain, one is forced to abandon all pretense and be the authentic self. There is no pretending when suffering; you are who you are and nothing more. Pain can also offer us connection. Being aware of our own vulnerabilities can make us more sensitive to the struggles of others. Our sense of superiority disappears, and we realize that what connects us is our woundedness, not the façade of strength. Pain also helps us understand reciprocity. When we are suffering profoundly, we often need the help of others. Because pain makes us selective about the ways in which we are willing to expend energy, sometimes all we have to offer in return is gratitude. But in that gratitude, there is an exchange, a call to relationship. In the

---

[3] Liz Crow, "A Certain Knowing," in *Inside Grief,* ed. Line Wise (Incline Village: Wise Press, 2001), 33. Reprinted by permission from Wise Press.

labyrinth of the psyche, there is the possibility that you can better know yourself, and perhaps even others, but often it is hard to see that while you are in it. And when it feels like the heart can no longer keep breaking, the natural movement is toward despair, or a dulling of feeling. Despair provides a necessary period of restoration and offers a final protection against the overwhelming loss. It is a descent into the dark.

In fairy tales and myths throughout the world, the dark signals a return to the instinctual self, the place of intuitive knowing and waiting. The dark is formless as it swallows, obscures, extinguishes all that is known. This state is externally represented in folktales as heroes or heroines suddenly find themselves on an island, or in a cave, or a tower, or a desert, or in an altered form (like an animal). There are wells, or deep pools, dark forests, and always ambiguity. Every crackle of a branch or rustling of a leaf signals potential danger. Not able to rely on our usual way of interpreting the surroundings, we are left with raw, unmediated inner knowing as a means to survival. It is in this place that one needs to learn to see with one's heart because what is essential cannot be understood with logic, or controlled by the ego.

The stripping away of our navigational tools, particularly clear sight, feels terrifying because we are in unknown (and unknowable) territory. It is during this time that many of us directly experience the shadow sides of ourselves. We may scream and rage and self-destruct. We may curl up into a little ball and not bother to get out of bed or bathe ourselves. This disheveled outward appearance may reflect the soul's desire to identify with the animal parts of ourselves—those parts that smell and bare fangs and burrow and hunt and *survive*. When we look in the mirror and see the crazed reflection staring back at us through deep, purple bags under our eyes, it is a signal that the ego is no longer steering. The soul knows that it is with reptilian, old brain consciousness that we must proceed inward.

Though a deeply disturbing time of stagnation, hopelessness, and meaninglessness, experiencing what St. John of the Cross called "The Dark Night of the Soul"[4] is an important part of the work of grief. It is in this deprived place that we meet "Lady Death,"[5] who always has two cups on her table—one that heals and one that kills.

Though we have masculine images of Death, such as The Grim Reaper, Death and its twin, regeneration, historically and cross-culturally have been most closely associated with the feminine. One of the earliest examples of this relationship is evidenced by figurines that were found from the Neolithic period (approximately 10,000 years ago). They are called "stiff, white ladies" and they were usually placed in gravesites. Made of bone, they had a well-defined pubic triangle and a birdlike face, sometimes with looming owl eyes.[6] The owl is significant in that it is comfortable in "night-consciousness." It has well-disguised feathers, nearly silent flight, eyes designed for acute perception in almost complete darkness, and the ability to hear the faintest of sounds. It is widely thought to be both the harbinger of death

---

[4] For an in-depth discussion of this topic, see Thomas Moore, *Dark Nights of the Soul* (New York: Gotham Books, 2004), and Linda Leonard, *Witness to the Fire: Creativity and Veil of Addiction* (Boston: Shambala, 1989), 227-242.
[5] Clarissa Pinkola-Estés, *Women Who Run With the Wolves* (New York: Balantine, 1997), 143.
[6] Marija Gimbutas, *The Language of the Goddess* (San Francisco: Harper-Collins, 1991), 198-199.

as well as an opportunity for communication with the spirit world.[7] For the Pimas and Kwagulths of North America as well as the Japanese, owls were believed to hold and transport the spirits of the dead to the next world. Conversely, owl feathers, among some Native American tribes, are thought to ensure an easy childbirth. For the Hopis, the burrowing owl is the god of the dead (called Kokongyam, which means "watcher of the dark").[8] As in the opening tale of Nyctea of the Pacific Northwest, among several North American tribes death itself is referred to as "crossing the owl's bridge." The owl is a symbol that transcends the material and the spiritual worlds, and can be seen as connecting the conscious and unconscious ones as well. It may be seen as one incarnation of "Lady Death."

Lady Death, as a transcendent figure, shows up in many guises in worldwide mythologies. In contemporary Mexico she is "Santa Muerte," both grandmother and "bitch."[9] She is revered particularly by the marginalized and those in prison, and she is said to enjoy offerings of tequila, cigarettes, and chocolate. She is symbolized in statues and images as a skeleton who can lovingly accept you complete with faults and grant you further life. Or she can be straight up with you and tell you it's your time. In Greek mythology, Artemis is not only the goddess of childbirth, but the overseer of quick and painless deaths. The Celts

---

[7] Gimbutas, *The Language of the Goddess*, 187.

[8] Webmaster, n.d. "Native American Indian Owl Legends, Meaning and Symbolism from the Myths of Many Tribes," http://www.native-languages.org/legends-owl.htm.

[9] Carmin Sesin, "Growing Devotion to Santa Muerte in U.S. and Abroad," http://www.nbcnews.com/news/latino/growing-devotion-santa-muerte-u-s-abroad-n275856.

have "The Lady of the Lake," who, legend describes, incubates the young Arthur in her castle under the water, allowing for his rebirthing into a developed sense of self. A most vivid expression of "Lady Death" comes to us from the Aztecs. Coatlicue[10] was said to be both the tomb and the womb. She wore nothing but a skirt of intertwined rattlesnakes and a necklace made of human hearts and hands. Her breasts were pendulous and hung down from too much suckling. Her fingers and toenails were sharp claws used to dig the graves of people she had devoured. In one incarnation, she was called Llamateuctli. This goddess wore a two sided mask—one on the front and one behind. Both had open mouths, sharp teeth, and bulging eyes. The front signified her death-wielding energies, and the other life-giving qualities. In another incarnation, she is La Llorona,[11] the mother who drowned her own children out of desperation when her husband left her for a younger woman. She weeps knee-deep in the river, caught between the world of the living and the dead, unable to enter the kingdom of heaven until she recovers the souls of the dead children. It is said that she often mistakes other children for her own and kills them. She sometimes appears with a pomegranate, each seed the heart of a child she took away.

In all her manifestations Coatlicue is associated with snakes. The snake as a symbol also holds the twin qualities of death and regeneration. In Mexico, the rattlesnake is said to be representative of poverty that, in turn, gets housed or swallowed up by a benevolent Earth. Other cultures also cite the death/rebirth

---

[10] Pinkola-Estés, *Women Who Run with the Wolves,* 210.
[11] Pinkola-Estés, *Women Who Run with the Wolves,* 326-327.

connection. In Egypt, snakes serve as an integrative symbol of transformation. It is that which sheds its skin and emerges into a new life. In ancient Greece, two snakes entwined around a wand was the emblem of Asklepius, the god of medicine and healing. The Aboriginal snake goddess Eingana[12] is said to be the mother of all water, animals and humans. She has a sinew attached to the heel of every creature, which is intertwined with the sinew of all of life. When she lets go, death ensues and your spirit re-enters the web of energy and may re-emerge in another creature. In Russia, one bylina, or poem that is chanted, relays that a knight and his wife make a pact that if one should die, the other will join the spouse in the grave. When the wife dies, the knight agrees to be placed in the coffin with her on the condition that he be given a rope attached to a church bell so he can ring it if he changes his mind. After being lowered under the earth, the knight lights a candle at midnight and sees that snakes have infested the coffin. He takes out his sabre and cuts off their heads, rubbing the decapitated but still writhing bodies all over his dead wife. She is miraculously restored to life and he rings the bell and they are rescued. Comparable symbols exist in virtually every culture's enduring stories. These beliefs speak to the experience of death and regeneration in the hands of Lady Death, who reminds us to sit in the ambivalence and confusion of this difficult time, and trust that there is no death without life and no life without death. She also tells you that you will not feel like this forever.

---

[12] Alexander Reed, *Aboriginal Myths: Tales of the Dreamtime* (Sydney: Reed New Holland, 2001).

Lisa

In preparation for THAT DAY, I had signed up for this grief workshop. I knew I needed something structured to keep me here, among the living. But when THAT DAY came, I couldn't go. I pulled the rope out from under the bed and put it over the beam in the bathroom. I put the stool in there and made sure that I could reach the loop that I had made. The kids were gone, and I had my notes very carefully prepared to lie out on the counter, and I arranged them over and over again. And I sat on the stool in the bathroom and I looked down at my feet. The black nail polish was chipped. Funny, but that's what held my attention as my mind careened into hell. I had survived so much—poverty, early sexual abuse, alcoholism, drug addiction. I had been sober for seven years and through so much counseling, but the voices were screaming—the blackness, sucking me down. I was the youngest of four girls. Four years ago, my oldest sister killed herself. Then, on the anniversary of her death, my second sister hung herself as well. Then, on the same day, THAT DAY, the third sister joined them. She took pills, though. Was it my turn? I was spinning, being sucked down. Just then the phone rang, and I heard a woman I knew asking me if I was going to go to the workshop today. I ran and picked up the phone and said, "YES! YES, I am going." And that was it. I went. I sat in the front row and I told my story. It was so quiet in the room. The people there were so kind, I'll never forget that. It made me feel as if I had one foot in this world while my other foot was dangling from the rope attached to the beam in the bathroom. And there was this man there in orange Crocs, who had lost his only connection/family in the world—an 18-year-old cat. He felt silly telling his story after mine and offered to leave. But it didn't matter. We all came around him and loved him just the same, and I felt companionship on this crazy, roller coaster of a journey. Ropes and Crocs and dead cats. I went from feeling so alone to feeling so connected. The more I go back and forth between these places, the more I trust that it will always change. And I don't have to get so stuck in one feeling.

Tenaya

When my 19-year-old son died of a gunshot wound to the head, it all happened so quickly. His friend called crying, and I went there. It never occurred to me to tell them to call 911, but I guess it doesn't matter. I'm not sure why I didn't think of that. He was lying in a puddle of his own blood. And his mouth was open. Like he was screaming. His eyes were open, too. My baby was scared. The last time I saw his face so covered in blood was the moment he was born, and his eyes looked just as wide. Bleeding into life and bleeding into death, a head soaked in red. My blood, his blood, the same blood. When the mortuary people came to take him and they zipped that plastic bag over his face, all the red went to white. I will never forget that moment. Just zip, and all gone. It was too soon, and I didn't get to be with him. I had a physical ache in my womb and I felt as if he was being ripped from me. My baby. At the viewing, I stayed near him until the very end. Everyone left except me and Ursula. The funeral director came and told me to say good-bye as he was closing up. And I kissed him and touched his hair and said,

"Sweetie, I am so sorry—so sorry." But when the man started to close the casket, I just couldn't take it. It was sudden, and my heart was beating and I wasn't thinking. I climbed in the casket with my son and laid down half next to him and half on top of him. When Ursula and the man tried to get me out, I pulled the top of the casket down on top of us. I was going to stay with him, that was all there was to it. They pulled, and as we fought, I bit my friend and lashed out with my fingernails. No one was going to take me from him. I was an animal. And I was fighting to die with my son. These days, I am fighting a different battle—to stay alive.

Who is this Lady Death who offers you two cups, one that kills you and the other that offers new life? She might be described as the queen of The Abyss. Leonard described it well: "In The Abyss is the paradox of all existence: joy mingled with terror, one's greatest loss as one's greatest possession, ignorance and knowledge, light and dark, ice and fire, life and death as One."[13] It is in that dark place that we find the integration of opposites, which are the elements of transformation. It is interesting that you are alive *and* dead in this place. At the same time, you are *neither* alive *nor* dead. You are being held in the *inbetween*. This fathomless, timeless place really challenges our sensibilities because we have been conditioned to be as logical as possible. It more resembles a dreamscape than a waking reality, and none of the old ways of being seem to work. During

---

[13] Linda Leonard, *Witness to the Fire: Creativity and Veil of Addiction* (Boston: Shambala, 1989), 234.

this confusion, Lady Death reminds us that our cups are filled with saltwater truth and there will be movement.

A good example of the transformative quality of being in the Abyss with Lady Death comes from Nepal. There is a particular species of the monkshood flower whose medicine is said to be so powerful that the same dose can either kill you or heal you. Shamans who are skilled in achieving transcendent states are called upon to administer it. The most important parts of the ritual are your belief in the flower as a curative agent and your respect for the cyclical nature of reality (life—death—life). Anecdotal reports of the flower's effects are that you feel as if you are being devoured as you are given new life. Lynne is one of those mothers who can speak about what that feels like. Her story is a chilling one, but it communicates the way the soul is at work, retrieving treasure from the underworld of the psyche, even when we feel we are being torn apart.

Lynne

I was a young bride who became pregnant soon after my marriage. Robert was handsome and so loving in the beginning. But, as my pregnancy progressed, he became increasingly cruel. He used to tell me I was fat and that nobody else would love me. He wouldn't let me handle my own money, and he was always controlling whom I could see. The night before my son was born, there was a particularly explosive exchange in which Robert pushed me against a wall and roughly shook me. I had the distinct sensation of feeling my baby turn abruptly in the womb, becoming breech. It was almost like Kenny was saying, "I'm not coming into this world."

My labor was difficult, but my son was born vaginally. I had a very special connection with him from the start. He was always such a sweet, sensitive boy. Even though I was still nursing, I became pregnant again right away. But Robert showed no pretense of being pleased. Now he was beating me regularly, telling me that I was worthless and ugly and didn't deserve to be a mother. He also told me that if I left him, he would hunt us down and kill us all.

I was terrified of Robert and his outrages, but I called the local domestic violence shelter. Kenny and I were held in protective custody and while we were living in a safe house, I gave birth to my daughter. I kept hoping that Robert and I would get back together, but all our attempts ended in screaming, shoving and more threats. The Women's Services people relocated us to another town.

For 18 years, my two children and I moved from town to town, changing our identities. Wherever we went, Robert eventually found us and threatened to kill us if we didn't come back. It was a terrifying way to live, always listening for that sound at the door—never knowing when he would appear or what he would do. But we made it—we made it for a long time.

When Kenny turned 18, he told me that he was interested in meeting his father. Everything in my body screamed out that this was wrong—you know when you get that feeling in your core that shouts NOOOOOO. But I realized that there was nothing I could do to stop him. Kenny was convinced that if he could just talk to his father, face to face, his understanding would grow, and they might be able to create a father/son relationship and lessen the fear that he, his sister, and I had been living with. I did believe that my son was especially gifted in connecting with people and that if healing were going to occur, this would be the way. So I told him that I didn't like it but that if he really needed to do it, I would be there for him. Kenny set up a meeting with Robert in a public park.

That night, I got a call from the police. Kenny had been shot three times. I knew that one bullet was meant for each of us.

The first time Lynne told this story, it was five years after Kenny's murder. Her voice was barely audible, shaking, and the sequence floated in a timeless emerging and fading of impressions. Her focus was very much on the trial and how difficult it had been to sit in a courtroom with Robert for the drawn-out legalities. It took two years to put him behind bars. She described the time since his imprisonment as a painful autopilot, where even the most basic of functions, like washing her hair, took a tremendous amount of energy. She mentioned several times that she would have been better off crawling into the casket with her son.

Each year, I invited Lynne to come hear the other mothers speak in my Death and Dying class and tell her story if she wanted to. Each year, she said she wasn't ready but came and spoke anyway. What was remarkable were the changes in the focus of the story through the years. Although she wasn't consciously aware of it, each time the experience was relayed, there was a shift in the emphasis of her feelings. In the beginning, it was raw pain; by the second and third time, defiant anger and indignation. The last time she spoke about how sad it must be to be Robert. She did not use the word "forgive," but she clearly demonstrated a move toward detachment and understanding of him as a mentally ill person. Her feelings toward Kenny had changed as well. Lynne thinks of Kenny as her special angel now, who is there to protect and guide her.

When talking later, she said that the annual speaking experience was the only overt marker of change that she had felt. She reflected that she could hear it in her own voice, the way that her pain was working itself over, making itself into something else.

Steven and Ondrea Levine, in their inspirational book on grieving, ask the question, "Who Dies?"[14] In many ways, you *are* psychologically dying alongside your beloved. We usually know ourselves most intimately in response to the person who calls forth particular traits in us. When that person no longer seems accessible, those parts of us that were stimulated appear to vanish along with our beloved. Where did those characteristics go? Are they still within us, or were they generated out of something that lies between ourselves and our loved ones?

Francine

I tried to visit Mom every other week but had been having a hard time managing even that. Alzheimer's had eaten away at her brain, her Lord & Taylor, carefully manicured identity. A person who was once such a lady, and so proud, greeted me

---

[14] Stephen and Ondrea Levine, *Who Dies?* (New York: Anchor Books, 1982).

with greasy, matted hair and spittle on her chin, last night's dinner on her nightgown. I spent a great deal of time making sure her bed was comfortable, adjusting the light in the room, taking care of her hygiene. I asked her over and over, "What can I do for you?" And, "Did you take your medication?" Sometimes she would answer, sometimes she wouldn't. I also decorated her room for all of the holidays, as if she still noticed the passing of time. One day one of the attendants came in, and I just erupted at her. Why hadn't anyone taken my mother to her nail appointment? How could they just let her go like this? Didn't anyone around here care? The poor woman just scurried out of the room, and I was left with my own rudeness and my increasing feelings of lack of control. I felt ashamed. I looked over at what was left of my mother, small and frail—birdlike, on the bed—and asked myself, "Why are you doing this?" Immediately, a list of reasons ran through my head. Because there is no one else to do it. Because she can't take care of herself. Because she won't remember to take her medication. Because these nursing home people are incompetent, they don't care. And it hit me. Underneath it all, I was doing this because I loved her. It was that simple. It wasn't about her nails or the crepe paper Halloween decorations or what kind of sheets she should have. So, I took a deep breath, feeling very foolish for having gotten it wrong for so long, and I sat down next to my mother. And I looked into her eyes. I really looked. And you know that line about eyes being the window to the soul. It's true, I felt it then. We had a moment where I thought we connected. And it was beautiful. This lasted for about 10 seconds. And then she said, "Who are you?" At first I wanted to scream, "I AM YOUR DAUGHTER!" But she just looked so curious in a naïve sort of way and I began, "I am….," but then I couldn't finish the sentence. Who was I if I wasn't my mother's daughter? And I began spinning, but I stayed quiet in myself. Ten seconds of connection helped me to stay in love. Slowly, other answers came to the surface. I am a friend and a worker and a neighbor and a caring person, and I am someone who likes Jane Austen novels and pistachio ice cream, and I am a wonderful tole painter. . .and . . . and. . . and. . .

Identity is a complicated construct and very tied to memory and relationships. We have enjoyed the privilege of witnessing our loved one's strengths and vulnerabilities, just as they have seen the essence of us. Without that mirror to show us our particularities and forgive our faults, we may grow confused.

Mary

I took a walk in the woods after a fresh blanket of snow in the high Sierra. Because of the new dusting on the path, patterns emerged. There were rabbit, raccoon, coyote, and bear tracks, among others. There was one place where a hawk had caught a mouse, and the faint outline of wings was imprinted in the snow. A bear walked toward the stream for a drink. A rabbit took cover from a hungry coyote. These events all occurred outside of my normal awareness. The snow became an emulsifying agent, much like developing fluid in a photo lab, and allowed me to see the images. I wondered if my husband is still here, but I have no ability to see or feel him. Are the love and parts of myself still there, inside of me, but outside of normal awareness? It takes some faith, and the right emulsifying agent, to make the invisible, visible.

It is important to have an external witnessing of the transformations that are occurring while you are in The Abyss, because it is nearly impossible to see them yourself. A good counselor or a wise friend might be a touchstone and emulsifier. Simply writing down your daily observations can be helpful. One very powerful way of tracking the movement is through attendance to your dreams.

Dreams

Dream images are often a good marker of the transformations that are taking place at the soul level during the darkest moments in bereavement. They may show you that the farewell in the material world can also be seen as a hello in the psychic realm.[15] The underlying assumption is that after bodily death, life may continue in a world of images, and we are being offered the opportunity to interact with them. Teresa's dream series illustrates this well.

As a dream image, Teresa's 16-year-old son Tito's presence has mirrored her grieving process. At first, he appeared in her dreams as a small child. This figure may express a desire to return to an earlier, more innocent time and may be representative of their parallel developmental journeys. She was truly in

---

[15] Greg Mogenson, *Greeting the Angels* (New York: Baywood, 1992), 18.

the infancy of her grief work, and like a child, did not have the context in which to situate her experiences. Next, Teresa had a series of telephone dreams. In them Tito would call and try to talk to her, but his mouth was full of tubes, and his speech all came out garbled. She was very alarmed and kept assuring him that "Mommy is here…I am right here." Telephone dreams may be a medium for conceptualizing the disembodied loved one.[16] There is communication but confusion as to the form on the other end of the line. In these dreams, Tito was trying to convey his presence, and she was offering her own, but connection seemed frustrating.

Approximately one year after his death, during what she reported as her deepest despair, Teresa had a dream in which she was walking through the grocery store. Tito's body was displayed in a meat case. It may have been a manifestation of her worst, unarticulated fear—that the end of material existence was the end of life and relationship. This dream image poetically expressed this fear for Teresa. She said of this time, "This was real hell now."

As Teresa grew more confident in her belief about the afterlife and in her and her family's ability to turn the situation into a positive experience, Tito's image in the dreams changed. He appeared older, more mature, and "just gorgeous." Teresa explained, "It was a healing step for me to see him just glowing. I finally had peace." She believed that Tito had shown himself to her as he was in heaven. She was quick to point out that even

---

[16] Deirdre Barrett, "Through the Glass Darkly: Images of the Dead in Dreams," *Omega: Journal of Death and Dying, 24,* (1992): 97-108.

though she had peace, the relationship never ends. She said, "That is *still* your baby, and your love only grows."

It has been a common finding among psychologists that dreams about the deceased are a healthy way to process feelings of abandonment.[17] The dream world presents to us those things that our egos are often not able to acknowledge. Early dreams, particularly after a violent or sudden death, may revolve around a replaying of the accident. These dreams are important in terms of the psyche's ability to situate the horrible imagery of the death and reflect the bereaved's trauma. During this initial period, these images can be symbolic, as in references to loss of control: You lose your car keys and you urgently need to be somewhere, you're being chased, there's a dead end, you leave the baby on top of the car, you are running in slow motion, trying to get away, or falling. You have no steering wheel, no brakes, or even no hands. Or they can directly reflect the overwhelming circumstances of the death. These dreams are especially present when there is a sudden or tragic loss. Marcia watched her husband's plane crash over and over. Teresa kept seeing her son on the hospital bed with tubes coming out of his mouth. Fiery car crashes may skip on the record player of our dreamscapes. This is the psyche's way of trying to make sense

---

[17] Barrett, "Through the Glass Darkly"; Patricia Garfield, *Dream Messengers* (New York: Simon & Schuster, 1997); George Pollack, *The Mourning Liberation Process* (Madison: International University Press, 1989); Beverly Raphael, *The Anatomy of Bereavement*, (New York: Basic, 1983); Stephanie Roeder, "Dreams and Grieving: A Qualitative Exploration of Dreams during the Period of Mourning Following the Death of Parent," *unpublished doctoral dissertation* (Boston: Boston University, 1981); Savine Weizman & Phylis Kamm, *About Mourning: Support and Guidance for the Bereaved* (New York: Human Sciences, 1985).

of the incomprehensible loss. In reviewing the circumstances, the psyche is trying to "place it" or make meaning out of it. These initial dreams are often extremely unpleasant. Though disturbing, the dreams may directly serve the bereaved and provide an environment for the safe expression of difficult feelings.

As another layer of consideration, prescientific cultures and modern tribal peoples have long-standing beliefs that the appearance of the deceased in dreams of the bereaved are actual visitations. Perhaps they can be both—something to help us through our feelings AND communications from our lost loved ones. Instead of seeing the dreams as an internally generated image or the presence of ghosts—they can be seen as something that is generated *between* the living and the dead.[18] This co-created image can be a rich source of information for understanding the dynamics in life as well as death.

Mike lost his life partner, Cliff to an aggressive form of brain cancer. In life, Mike had been the responsible one, while Cliff provided playful, boyish energy. In death, that relationship changed and both men evolved. The dream space offered a continuation of interaction and an environment for the resolution of issues.

Mike

At first I couldn't tell if my dreams were some sort of wish fulfillment. I wanted him there *so bad.* But over time I thought,

---

[18] Kimberly Bateman, "The Appearance of the Deceased in Dreams of the Bereaved: A Case of Co-Individuation," *unpublished doctoral dissertation* (Carpinteria: Pacifica Graduate Institute, 1999).

maybe if I stop fighting, maybe it will be a comfort to me. I was running, running at that time because I didn't want to stop and hear the echo in my brain, an empty echo like in a room when nothing's there. I didn't want to hear the hollowness so I filled myself with my own work. The first lucid dream I had about Cliff occurred about 10 months after his death. I was on Market Street and I saw him on the street in the Castro headed for another meeting. It was really him. I was elated and I wasn't going to hear that echoing silence because he was there! I was stunned. I was happy. He hadn't gone. He wanted to show me that he wasn't gone. Later, I began to realize he was still with me. He would show up in my dreams and he always came around when I was in conflict. He would just arrive, and we would talk. He would not "talk" back, but there would be a knowing. I had an answer. At first these interactions seemed like replays of memories. But then I realized that these were new issues, and we hadn't talked about them before. And the most stunning thing was that Cliff was maturing. He was no longer the impish, impulsive boy. I used to be the rational one, and now I found that I was freer to be playful, while he took on the role of the wise sage. The Cliff who appeared in my dreams was grown up. Nothing is tangible, I just know that somehow, I am still in relationship. It's a shared thing. I just know there is balance.

Soon after a significant loss, it is common to have dreams where the person appears and seems "just fine." There is often a knock at the door, or you are in a public place and your lost loved one just appears. Sometimes you are on a bus, or the loved one is sitting at your dining room table. For Mike, Cliff just innocently showed up on the street. Often our first response is confusion. "What are you doing here?" Or, "Don't you know that you are dead?" But, we are usually very happy to reconnect and awake feeling as if we have received a visitation. In later dreams, it is also common for the dead to have messages for us. Cliff appeared most in Mike's dreams when he had something to sort out and needed advice. Other types of messages may be in the form of apologies or the reflection of deep pain. Christine's husband died in an airplane accident while doing a military exhibition, leaving her with a $2000-a-month mortgage, no job, and a 5-year-old daughter.

Christine

In my dreams Mark would drive up in his truck, and I don't know why, but he would always ring the doorbell. He'd come in and hug our daughter, Holly. He'd be in his flight suit and say, "I'm so sorry you've had to go through all of this." In another series of dreams Mark would show up and say, "I feel so bad, Christine, I really didn't mean for this to happen." In these dreams I was so relieved, this huge weight was lifted off my shoulders. And knowing who he was, he probably would have felt terrible about what I was going through. I am not unsure that they weren't manifestations of his spirit saying, "I'm sorry this has happened." About a year later, my dreams took on a different theme. I used to dream about his body a lot, his physical body. It was so real to me. While I was married, I never really had sexual dreams, but after he died, very sexual. Mark ended up taking care of me in many ways. I had a lot of conversations with him about Holly. I would be upset about something and I would say, "OK, Mark, what should we do?" And later, in her teenage years I would say, "You'd better help out here." I didn't receive direct answers, but it was more of a knowing and things would happen. I believe Mark had a role in guiding me toward my current husband, who was Mark's best friend. Even though I am very happily married, I am always happy to see Mark. He's very real to me.

Later in the grieving process, it is also common to have dreams of the deceased that include a farewell hug, gifts, or messages of a departure. The deceased may say, "I am OK, and I have to go now," and generally inspire peace in the bereaved. Amy's dream series illustrates the full development from the appearance, to messages, to departure.

Amy

My 21-year-old brother died in a rock-climbing accident. In the first dream, I saw him sitting on a bus heading to a ski resort. It was so weird that he just appeared, and I was so happy to see him. About a year later, I dreamt I found these snow caves on the backside of NorthStar and rappelled down into one. I was walking through a labyrinth, and at the end was this room. Jerry was sitting in a rocking chair in front of a small fire. He had changed, and he didn't look well. He had long, scraggly hair and gnarled fingernails. I said to him, "WHAT are you doing here?" He said, "You have to tell Mom to let me go." In the next dream, I received a telephone call from Jerry. I asked him what it was like where he was. He said, "It's all MUSIC," and I was so happy that he was in such a beautiful place. In the next dream, Jerry was sitting at my dining room table and got up to leave. I became very upset, and he said, "Let me show you something that's in your own house." I followed him up the staircase, but we went up and up and up, well past the confines of my own house. There were ghostlike figures dressed in 18th-century garb passing us. When we got to the top, all the people who I knew who had died were sitting around playing parlor games. Jerry said, "This is in your house, and you can visit anytime you like." Jerry looked vibrant and healthy in this dream. In the last dream I had of Jerry, I was sitting beside a pond as the sun was setting. There were gorgeous orange-red, spotty clouds. Jerry's friend was beside me, and she said, "That's Jerry now, his energy has changed." I wasn't sad, it was more of a peaceful feeling, and I looked up in the sky with tears of joy and thought, "My God, you're beautiful, you really are."

There can definitely be awareness of beauty in this great pain. But, the dissolution of identity can be terrifying, and the unspeakable Raven black void that you feel inside can be agony. Just agony. No one wants to sit with Lady Death. She is ugly. She is greedy. She smacks her greasy lips and touches you with gnarled, yellow fingernails in the most uncomfortable places.

But it is only in surrendering to Lady Death that you are offered the other cup. The cup that is like rain on parched ground. The one that portends your soul retrieval. There is a Chinese saying, "A sincere heart can make a stone blossom."

"Yet, no matter how deeply I go down into myself/my God is dark/and like a webbing made of a hundred roots, that drink in silence."[1]

Rainer Maria Rilke

5

Stuck in the Abyss

The Tlingit story continues by recounting that the chief "still grieved greatly." The truth here is that one can do all the work—protect and support one's self, express rage and be cared for, sit with Lady Death, explore the big questions of meaningfulness and life and death—but it *still hurts.* Suffering can become a constant companion. A spiritual destitution may descend and the story becomes stagnant.

In the mythological realm, a good storyteller is able to situate experiences in the greater context of natural rhythms and an overriding sense of something bigger than individual angst. There is always another chapter, and Death is not seen as the end of anything. But in our personal worlds we often find ourselves feeling "stuck" on a certain page, unable to attune ourselves with any rhythm, be it internal or distant. No storyteller arrives to situate anything. Death feels like the end of everything. The knots of grief, instead of being slowly unraveled,

---

[1] Rainer Maria Rilke. "Poems from the French," *The American Poetry Review,* 3-3. 1973.

serve as something substantial to "hold on to." There can be a tragic sweetness in this feeling, in that by staying in pain we also are reminded that we have loved deeply. But sometimes we find ourselves clinging desperately to those knots and feelings as soul-defining compulsions, and it no longer serves us. This Finnish folk tale describes this predicament.[2]

The Spouses

Once there was a man and a woman who lived together in peace and harmony and who were as fond of each other as it is possible to be. One day the man said to his wife, "When I die, you will surely find another man."

"And you will surely find another woman," the wife replied. "You will not stay single forever."

But neither the man nor the woman believed the other, and so they decided to make a pact that neither one would remarry should the other one die.

As it happened, not long after that, the woman died. At first the man lived without a woman because he had no desire to marry again. But after some time passed he thought, "Why should I go on mourning like this? I am going to get married again." And indeed, he soon found himself another woman. Just as he was about to go and meet the bride, who was waiting for him by the church, he had an idea. "I shall visit my wife, bid her farewell,

---

[2] August von Löwis of Menar, Finnische und estnische Volksmärchen (Jena: Eugen Diederichs, 1922): 75-76. Retrieved from http://www.zeno.org/nid/2000784185X

and ask the dead woman to forgive me," he thought. And so he went to her grave, knelt down, and said, "Forgive me! I am going to a wedding. I am marrying again."

At this, the grave opened up and his wife's spirit called out to him. "Come, come. Don't be afraid, come here," she said, beckoning him. "Don't you remember what we promised each other? That whoever survives wouldn't get married again?" Then she talked him into climbing into the grave with her. "Will you have some wine?" she asked him as they were both sitting in the coffin, offering him a glass. After drinking, he wanted to leave, but she begged him saying, "Stay here a little while. Let us have a good talk!" Then she poured him a second glass of wine and he drank again. After this, he stood up to go again, but she insisted he stay and talk longer. "Do not go yet," she implored. And so the husband lingered on.

Meanwhile, the pastor was holding a prayer service at the church, for it was assumed that the man had fallen to his death. The bride-to-be, having waited and waited, finally returned to the home of her parents.

After the man's wife gave him a third glass of wine, she finally allowed him to leave the grave. "Go now!" she said. So the man left. When he arrived at the church, the pastor was no longer there. All the wedding preparations had been taken away, and he himself had grown as gray as an old hoopoe. He had been in the grave for thirty years.

—◆—

The story enacts being "stuck in the abyss" in a very concrete way. It speaks to the profound juncture in which most bereaved people find themselves—to live in relation only to the dead or integrate the experience, find a way to continue to love, and carry on in the world of the living. The story begins with the express desire for the couple's relationship to stay exactly as it has been—peaceful and harmonious. In this sentiment, there is a recognition of the beauty of innocence. Death, as the instigator of separation and knowledge, forces the couple to cross the threshold, and they are asked to come to terms with the new state of affairs. For deeply connected people, it can feel like the Garden of Eden has been ruptured. A most vital connection has been lost; it is almost like being orphaned.

The Orphan archetype resonates with those who have suffered the loss of their original ground, which often comes in the form of relationships. This pattern of abandonment (and subsequent reconnection) has been described in stories throughout the centuries. Moses was abandoned in a reed basket in a river. Romulus and Remus were discarded and later nursed by a wolf. The Ugly Duckling's egg rolled into the wrong nest. Huck Finn was abused by his alcoholic father before he staged his own death and set out with Jim on the raft. A pivotal moment in Batman's life is when both of his parents are murdered by a mugger. Superman, Snow White, Cinderella, Pinocchio, Little Orphan Annie, Luke Skywalker, and Harry Potter—orphans, every one. It is strange how their disenfranchisement is both painful and sacred; how they are endowed with special gifts, but how we can all relate to their hurting. It is important that the theme of absence and isolation gives way to growth and reconnection to love in each of these stories. In stark contrast, "The Spouses" story serves as much more of a cautionary tale. When one is bound by the old stories (the "pact") and seduced into being spiritually fed only by the deceased, we find that we are metaphorically climbing into the coffin right alongside our loved one. People who are stuck in the abyss are familiar with this feeling.

Interestingly, the husband begins by heeding his instincts. He mourns and then, after some time, feels the pull to engage in living again by marrying. But he feels guilty that he cannot honor the promise he made to his wife and believes that returning to the grave (his past) is more important than keeping his commitment to the bride-to-be (his future). The memory of the dead and the desire for his former peace and harmony are compelling. She calls to him and offers him some wine, also known as a "spirit," inviting him to transcend the body, become less conscious, and join her in the imaginal. It is a seductive bargain, and it cost him dearly.

Receiving food or drink from the dead is tricky business in folktales. In Greek mythology, Persephone is abducted by Hades, the god of the dead/underworld. This causes Demeter, Persephone's mother and goddess of fertility and agriculture, to mourn and make the land go barren. After Persephone is rescued, it is determined that because she ate six pomegranate seeds while in captivity, she is bound to the world of the dead for six months out of the year. Hence the reoccurrence of winter, as her mother grieves afresh each year. Metaphorically, this shows that we must exercise discrimination in determining what will sustain us and what will not. More specifically, it asks us to address the question of *who* will feed us. The dead, though loved and honored, can no longer sustain us in the old way. It is also important to note that the tale does not discourage relationship with the dead; it warns us about a certain kind of relationship—one in which we forgo the world of the living to tend to unhealthy stories we have about the dead, or one in which we deny that we are incarnate beings. These "stories" can show up with many different themes and twists.

Eve

When my husband died quite suddenly of a stroke, I couldn't believe I was supposed to go back to work in three days. Three days, three years, three lifetimes wouldn't make it better. Over the last six years it is as if pain has become my constant companion and I don't know who I am without it. There are a few moments in the morning when I first wake up and I forget what happened, but then the weight presses down on me with suffocating intensity, and it is like starting all over again. Sometimes I catch myself thinking, *my pain is as deep as my love.* And then, because I love him so, I wonder if I will ever stop hurting. If I do, does that mean that I no longer love him? Does not hurting mean a betrayal on my part? And no one seems to understand this, and everyone is so tired of me being sad. I don't have anyone to talk to.

Tom

I am a good man, a principled man. I go to church every Sunday and I don't lie or steal or cheat. I keep my word. For me the rules are simple. If you are a good person, good things happen to you. If you are a bad person, bad things happen to you. It says so in the Bible. My 18-year-old son died in a way that I am ashamed to even say, and that was the hardest thing I've ever lived through. My wife and I have not been able to talk about it. About 15 years later, a young man who looked exactly like our son showed up on our doorstep. He said he was Aaron's son. Ellen and I just cracked open with joy, and neither one of us could stop crying. And here's this poor boy just standing on the step thinking we are out of our minds. He stayed with us for a few days, and we loved every moment of it. His laugh and his walk and his sense of humor were just like his father, our son, and it almost felt as if he had returned to us. We were so happy. On the last day, Ellen went to wake him because he didn't come down to breakfast. She found him exactly the way we had found his father. He had done it to himself on purpose. I still don't think that bad things happen to good people and so I am sure that I have done something wrong on this earth. I don't know what that something is, but I carry barbed wire in my heart all the time for whatever it might be.

Elva

I drink almost every night now. I don't want to be in my own head, don't want to hear the mind talk. I should not have let her go in the car with those boys. Bad Mother. Failure at the only important job in my life. Bad Mother. I deserve to hurt, and when I am not hurting in my head, I am hurting in my body. In some ways there is satisfaction in being punished, as I so deserve it. I am humiliated.

Gena

I have five boys. And you know how, as a mother, your heart and attention always go toward the one who is in trouble, the one who needs you most. It's instinctual, to be with your child when he is having a hard time because that is what your heart tells you to do. When my oldest son had his accident, it seemed like the most natural thing in the world. I had to go with him, to be with him in the next dimension. He needed me, and I wanted to cross over to be with him so I could help him wherever he was.

Nicole

My daughter died from a disease that could have been prevented had we immunized her. She was nine. I began with small procedures. I had my chin tucked, and then liposuction on my thighs. Next I had an abdominoplasty (tummy tuck), and that was quite a major surgery. With each surgery, I felt good for a little while, and then the tension would rise, and I felt the need to improve myself, to control death. I have now spent many thousands of dollars improving my body and during the last one, my husband said I looked like an animal that had been butchered. Age and deterioration is not going to get me. It's not going to win.

···❖···

We hear, with heartache, the stories these bereaved people are telling themselves and know that however convoluted they sound, they reveal real issues. Our first instinct is to solve these issues. We want to reason with them— "Bad things happen to good people all the time!" Or "You are hurting enough, stop hurting yourself." Or "Please stay in the world of the living, you are needed here." But logic rarely works where emotions are concerned, and these beliefs make perfect sense to those who are feeling the fear. Remember that the stories are unconscious ways to try to regain a sense of control in a situation that feels overwhelming and scary. Or more extremely, to rationalize something that is not rational—death itself.

These strategies can be symptoms of existential or spiritual desperation. We are often so frightened of death and the ensuing desperation and pain that a great deal of time and energy is spent rationalizing or resisting it, or being afraid that it will stay this way forever. These approaches further compound the suffering and don't allow us to really sit with the experience. For example, Elva's strategy of drinking alcohol to deaden her awareness just delays the processing and incorporation of the experience. And we know that drinking to allay any intense feeling is a bit like turning off the "check engine" light on the car's dashboard. The reminder of the deep pain may be removed temporarily, but there is still something wrong with the engine. Use of any psychoactive drug, from sleeping pills to marijuana, helps to ignore the symptoms, but it most certainly will not fix anything in any meaningful way. The chemicals actually create more problems than the original stressor, in that they lower the immune system, are dehydrating, and can inhibit the ability to have quality inter-personal relationships. Alcohol, painkillers, sleep aids, valium, etc., are depressants and are symptoms of the desire for control and a fear of lack of connectivity. Unfortunately, these strategies don't address the insecurity underneath, and that actually makes it worse by not acknowledging the fear.

And what is the ultimate fear in bereavement? It is that we are unsafe, alone, unloved, that we will not survive, that our loved one was just a physical body who is now gone forever and there is no meaning to it all, and that our intense love will never be returned. We have been conditioned to relate only to the physical, brainwashed to believe that attachment brings satis-faction. We cling to life and deny its regenerative twin, death, which are really two sides of the same coin.

A story from Greek mythology that speaks of some of these existential fears and, in particular, the sadness of love not re-turned, is that of Echo and Narcissus.[3]

Echo falls deeply in love and is subsequently rejected by the lovely Narcissus. She is said to be so saddened by this blow that she pines away until she dies of grief, becomes one with the moun-tain stone, and is nothing but a voice. Later, the gods put a curse on Narcissus, willing him to fall in love with someone who could never love him back. He sees his own reflection in a pool of water, which he confuses with a water sprite. He is struck by its dazzling beauty. He bends down to kiss his vision, sees it rising toward him

---

[3]Ovid, "Echo and Narcissus," in trans. Stanley Lombardo, *Metamorphoses* (Indianapolis: Hacket, 2010): 79-81.

and then watches it disappear as his lips touch the water. He frustratingly repeats this action over and over and is freshly disappointed each time. He becomes so frightened to have the image of his beloved (himself) disintegrate that he eventually lies by the pool, gazing at his own reflection in pain. Narcissus, like Echo, died of grief. His body disintegrated, and what was left in its place was a beautiful flower, his namesake, the Narcissus. It can often be found growing at the edges of pools of water.

So much of loving is about a deep craving for connection through accurate mirroring. We need to know who we are as reflected by our loved ones. Jane is her sister's twin. Linda is her son's caretaker. Betty is Walt's wife. Pasquale is Tito's father. Gordon is Janeen's deepest romantic love. Almost all grief begins narcissistically. We will *miss them terribly.* We miss how they made us feel and who we thought we were when we were with them. Chad reflected parts of my mother that could laugh at the silliness of the "establishment." Walt reminded Betty that she is a valued, hardworking, and devoted partner who makes the best chicken cutlet. Tito helped Pasquale recognize what a loving and supportive father he is; a cheering, familiar face at ball games, the calm voice of reason in a hectic world. Janeen knows herself as Gordon's "Iron Rose" in pretty shoes. She feels her beauty and her solidity through him. It is no wonder that we are so sad. The image projected back to us as we gaze into Narcissus' pool is unrecognizable. We reach out to touch, but the image of our longing disintegrates, both internally and externally. The dazzling beauty is hard to see. It feels OK to rest a while at the bottom of the hole and be "swallowed up."

Mothers and fathers who have lost children, in particular, are susceptible to the toxicity of this complex. It is hard for parents to imagine their children as autonomous from them (especially in death) because developmentally, children are in such a vulnerable and dependent state. Couple this truth with the enormous amount of emotional, physical, and financial energy that parents have invested into their children. It is hard to untangle who you are from who they are. It's nearly impossible. And so the story can become stagnant, and rumination, rather than being an act of creation (in piecing together the stories of you and the deceased) becomes rigid.

To sit with the image of Echo is to describe intense grief well—to feel as if your identity has disintegrated and you are removed from the world, a mere echo of the person you used to be. Like Narcissus, love is out of reach, intangible. You no longer have the capacity to imagine anything for yourself or for your loved one. In some eschatological systems, such as the pre-Christian Central American mythologies, true hell is defined as the inability to feel anything, either good or bad, for eternity. No fresh images break through. You are left in a dark, insulated place of numbness with no capacity for imagination. It is no wonder that the husband willingly crawls back into the grave with his deceased wife.

A Note on Suicide

A particularly difficult type of madness often occurs in the aftermath of a suicide. It can feel like grief on steroids. Among other things, we are so wholly conditioned to believe that life is good and death is bad, it is unbelievable that someone would choose to enter the space of death willingly. It is inconceivable that our love has not been strong enough to hold someone in this place. It is truly a complicated grief. Some of the unique reactions to suicide might include intensified guilt as well as anger at the perceived selfishness.

Guilt

When a loved one chooses to die, it may bring up our own profound sense of failure. We replay the situation over and over in some attempt to control what we cannot. We want to undo it, take it back, press restart. The bereaved can be riddled with questions—"What could I have done? How could I have changed it? Did I spend my time well? Did I love enough? Why wasn't my love enough? Why didn't I see the signs? Why didn't they come to me for help?" Followed by, "I should have known," "if only I were closer," and "if only….." At the most core level, we are brought face to face with our own impotence. This rumination serves the fantasy that it could have been changed. But of course, control is an illusion. The death is not anyone else's responsibility. It is only the responsibility of the person who chose it. Ironically, when we stay in the place of guilt, we are reconstructing the mental anguish that was expressed in the suicide itself. In some ways, it may serve to keep the bereaved identifying and in connection to the deceased. But that connection is hellish.

David

Every home needs a gun in case someone is threatening your family. It was a good idea, and I was being a protective dad. But it ended up being the dumbest move of my entire life. My beautiful boy Ryan used that gun to kill himself. As soon as I heard the news and how he did it, I knew it was all my fault. Could there be anything dumber? I was not a good dad. In fact, I was the worst kind of dad—irresponsible. Dumb. And from that moment on, my days were a living hell. Why hadn't I talked to him more? Why didn't I know? Could I have been worse of a failure?

⟡

Anger at "Selfishness"

In the aftermath of suicide, people often ruminate and sift through a myriad of reactions. One common thought is, "He or she was so SELFISH." By selfish, it is usually meant that, "they were not thinking of ME, or their children, or the people who loved them." And those thoughts are correct. They weren't thinking of you. They were thinking many other things, such as: "I am consumed with pain and I need it to change. I need to take back control. I feel no spark, no will to live, I am already dead. I am overwhelmed and suffering." When one is consumed with pain, he or she is incapable of thinking of others because the feelings fill them. Imagine a person in an accident and who has punctured a lung and shattered a leg. While they are lying there, would they be thinking, "I wonder how my husband is doing," or "I should send my mother a card"? The only thing on that person's mind would be how to alleviate the suffering. So, instead of saying he or she was so "selfish" we can remind ourselves that our loved one's mind was weary and his or her heart was frightened and hopeless. The dead most need our compassion, not our judgment. The living most need our compassion, not our judgment. Still, these stories we tell ourselves that keep us separate from loving, like, "it's all my fault," can be very compelling.

A folk tale that appears in many forms throughout northern European countries is "The Snow Queen." The story lends some insight into this "frozen" state of stories that are no longer fluid—like if you stop being in pain, you stop loving, or that bad things only happen to bad people, or that you deserve to be punished, or that you should never love again. Other common thoughts are: "I am a failure," and "Why me?" These stories become entrenched, like a rutted-out road, and it is hard to take another route. When imagination cannot break through and attachment to the physical body is confused with the more universal feeling of the love that vivifies it, life is bleak, indeed. As an example, if the television set breaks, the signal doesn't cease to exist, just the physical conductor that channeled it does. No fresh images come through, and one can become tricked into thinking that the box itself was the generator.

In "The Snow Queen," the title itself is provocative and relates directly to emotional possibilities in mourning. Snow as an image transforms the landscape as it blankets. It is cold, yet it also presents an insulating layer that protects plants and animals from harsh temperatures. A single snowflake is crystalline beauty, a delicate and unique art form. It is a balance of elements—solid, liquid, gas, and when an individual joins the collective, it has force. In holding these dual images together —a snowflake on the tongue and the rumbling power of an avalanche—it can be like emotions, alternatingly tingling or delicious—and overwhelming.

Add the Queen, and there is now an otherworldly, cold figure, the distant feminine, who sucks the emotions and life out while offering her brittle beauty. There is no comfort there. She is shell-like, devoid of feeling. The woman whose own intense wounding has shut her down, made her indifferent. And yet, she has authority, this queen. She rules, as in "The Lion, the Witch and the Wardrobe," with cruelty and the capacity to render one motionless with the wave of her hand.

Frozen feelings, frozen creativity. No fresh images breaking through.

"The Snow Queen" tale begins with a scene in which a troll has invented a special mirror:

Long before your father and mother were born, in places far to the north, everyone knew that if things went wrong it was the fault of the trolls. Trolls usually live near bridges and have exceptional hearing, strong jaws, very sharp teeth and long arms that are well-suited to grabbing unsuspecting passers-by. You know they are lurking about because of the smell of wet dog, rotten wood, and decaying fish all mingled together. They say that trolls are mean-spirited because they are both slow-witted, and afflicted with the most ravenous of hungers, attacking flocks of sheep as their favorite meal. Sometimes they have even been known to satisfy themselves with the flesh of people. But mostly, they spend their time trying to make humans miserable—you see, they hate them so.

One day, the most evil of all the trolls was exceedingly pleased with himself. He had invented a very unique mirror. This mirror had the power to make anything beautiful and good become distorted, and appear repulsive in the reflection. Thus, the fairest of maidens would look blemished and deformed; the most noble of warriors, cowardly and weak; the kindest, most true of friends, like rats in a refuse pile. Even pure and good thoughts elicited a negative response from the mirror, and it would break into a malevolent grin.

One day, the trolls decided to have some fun. They gathered around the large mirror, grabbed ahold of the edges and flew up towards heaven to taunt God himself. Up and up they went, holding the edges of the special mirror, snickering as they climbed. The closer they got to God, the more the mirror reacted—a malevolent grin turning into a giggle, and then a full, evil laugh. The mirror shook so hard with a sinister cackle that the trolls lost their grip. The mirror fell and broke into a billion little slivers.

Andersen's[4] version describes what happens next:

Some of the splinters were as tiny as grains of sand and just as light, so that they were spread by the winds all over the world. When a sliver like that entered someone's eye it stayed there; and the person, forever after, would see the world distorted, and only be able to see the faults, and not the virtues, of everyone around him, since even the tiniest fragment contained all the evil qualities of the whole mirror. If a splinter should enter someone's heart—oh, that was the most terrible of all! —that heart would turn to ice.

Being caught in unhealthy stories about ourselves or others is very much like having a little piece of the troll's glass lodged

[4] Hans Christian Andersen. "The Snow Queen," Hans Christian Andersen: The Complete Fairy Tales and Stories (New York: Anchor, 1974), 235.

in your eye and, more extremely, your heart. Everything becomes distorted. "It's not fair," is one of those stories. "It's all my fault," is another one. "If I stop hurting, that means I stop loving." "If only I had….." Sometimes the thoughts designed to help us survive hurt us the most. You may fall into some of the common traps of believing that your loss will become a never-ending pattern of bad things to happen, or dwell only on ways in which you have failed your loved one.

Cory

I backed over my own child in the driveway. "I looked," is what I say to myself over and over as I replay that moment for the thousandth time. "I looked," again and again and again.

I did look. And I keep looking. Eighteen years later I'm still looking over my right shoulder for a blond-haired boy. All I can see is self-loathing and doubt. Failure. I have recently been diagnosed with a degenerative neurological disorder, and I know it is related to the demons in my head. At least I will be with my son soon and be able to tell him I'm sorry.

Jo-Jo

I was just watching T.V., that's all. And there was nothing special on. I was fully awake and at some point I thought, "Where is Clara?" It hadn't been that long. It really hadn't. I looked in her room and the garage. I couldn't find her and my heart began racing. I called out, "CLARA!" and I began running like a madwoman around the house. Then I saw it. The back slider open and her little footprints in the snow. But where had she gone? The top was on the hot tub, but her tracks stopped on the top step. I opened the cover and there she was in the water. She must have lifted it just enough to crawl under. But she was gone. My little girl was gone. It's been nine years and I honestly don't feel much at all anymore. I am the one who really died that day.

Frozen feelings, frozen creativity. No fresh images breaking through. "The Snow Queen" tale begins with the story of the troll's glass then explains how the heroine, Gerda, must go into the wide world and undergo a series of tasks and trials to locate her beloved friend, Kai. He had been stricken with a piece of the troll's mirror in his heart and a sliver in each of his eyes. He had also been abducted by the Ice Queen.

When Gerda finally finds Kai, he is sitting in a great snow hall, under the northern lights on a frozen lake that is called the "Mirror of Reason," which The Snow Queen calls the finest and only mirror that is worthy. He is arranging pieces of ice, shuffling them around and around, trying to form a word that will earn him his freedom, the whole world and new pair of skates. The Ice Queen says that he must spell the word "Eternity," but he often forgets this and so appears frozen and dumbfounded, pushing the pieces this way and that. Anderson relays:[5]

---

[5] Andersen, The Snow Queen, p. 260.

Little Kai was blue—indeed, almost black—from the cold, but he did not feel it, for the Snow Queen had kissed all feeling of coldness out of him, and his heart had almost turned into a lump of ice. . .

Little Gerda. . . she saw Kai! She recognized him right away, and ran up to him and threw her arms around him, while she exclaimed jubilantly: "Kai, sweet little Kai. At last I have found you."

But Kai sat still and stiff and cold; then little Gerda cried and her tears fell on Kai's breast. The warmth penetrated to his heart and melted both the ice and the glass splinter in it.

Kai burst into tears and wept so much that the grains of glass in his eyes were washed away. Now he remembered her and shouted joyfully: "Gerda! Sweet little Gerda, where have you been so long? And where have I been?" Kai looked about him. "How cold it is, how empty, and how huge!" And he held onto Gerda, who was so happy that she was both laughing and crying at the same time. It was so blessed, so happy a moment that even the pieces of ice felt it and started to dance, and when they grew tired they lay down and formed exactly the word for which the Snow Queen had promised Kai the whole world and a pair of new skates.

Gerda kissed him on his cheeks and the color came back to them. She kissed his eyes and they became like hers. She kissed his hands and feet, and the blue color left them and the blood pulsed again through this veins. He was well and strong. Now the Snow Queen could return, it did not matter, for his right to his freedom was written in brilliant pieces of ice.

According to the Snow Queen tale, when troll's glass gets stuck in the eye and/or the heart—when frozen in this way of relating—relationship and tears become the vehicle to salvation. When the Snow Queen declares that the mirror of reason is the finest and only worthy mirror in the world, anyone who has grieved knows that she is mistaken. Death makes no sense. The story reminds us that logic alone will not carry us. It shows that it is through the expression of deep pain that we become connected and healing is affected. We are being asked to become well-versed in confronting those dark parts of ourselves. And we usually find that as soon as we let go of trying to manipulate suffering, we are free to recognize what's going on, acknowledge where the feelings came from, and lovingly sit with them to see what they are asking.

Jane

When my twin sister was killed, I felt as if someone had encased me in concrete. Thick concrete. And there was a rumbling of feeling inside that I could not, would not let out. It was just festering there. If I did let it out, it would be a deadly force that would overwhelm me and drown everything around me. Annihilation. I lived like this for almost two years, and the only place I allowed myself to cry was in the car by myself. These tears just kind of leaked out, and I didn't want to really let it go, because I wouldn't be able to drive. One day, I went down and sat on the end of the Dollar Point dock on Lake Tahoe. It was near sunset and a perfectly calm day. There was not a wisp of wind, and the lake was like a blue-green mirror. I asked God if I was going to survive this. I told him that I couldn't take it anymore and was very tempted to lean forward and fall into the lovely, dark, deep water and die. It stayed perfectly calm, and he was not answering. I began to cry, softly at first, but then loudly. I cried as I had not allowed myself to cry, from the very center of my being. I felt a cracking at the base of my pelvis, and it was a physical sensation, like fissures in my skin. This feeling spread to my stomach and chest, and finally my face. It was as if light had been trapped inside and was trying to leak out through the fissures. Each fissure felt like a cut, an open wound that hurt. Little lines of pain all over. Just when the burning increased to the point of intolerability, a very gentle breeze picked up over the lake. I could see the ripples in the distance in a massive, 10-mile line of movement. As I looked up, I realized it was coming toward me and I waited. The wind hit my wet cheeks and my eyes, now raw from crying. It is hard to describe, but the heat from all the fissures was instantly cooled by the gentle fingers of that breeze. The concrete had broken into a million pieces, and the light could now come out without hurting. And that light was met with a soothing response. I think God answered me. I knew I would be OK.

Cynthia

At my son's funeral, it felt as if everyone was looking at me. They wanted to see that I was OK, and I wanted so badly to comfort them, to not frighten them. I needed to appear "strong," and I did not want the pity. I felt so much emotion welling up, but it didn't seem like the right place to let it all out. No place is the right place to let it all out, it seems. Isn't that weird, that we're not even supposed to cry at funerals. I guess we are really not supposed to cry in front of anyone unless we pay them $120/hour. Well the feelings leaked out my eyes every time I went in the car by myself. And then I would worry that my face was all red and that people would know. I lived like this for a very long time. After several years of holding this in my body and feeling almost as if I couldn't breathe, I decided to participate in a grief ritual at a retreat center. I was terrified that the hole would open up and just swallow me. That I would fall and fall and fall and never get to the bottom. We put objects and pictures of our loved ones in a shrine and then we began telling our stories. The woman next to me wailed and wailed. And a strange thing happened. I wasn't afraid. If she could do it, I could do it. When I looked at her, I felt nothing but deep compassion. When it was my turn, I broke completely open and cried rivers. Rivers and rivers and rivers. I imagined these rivers carrying my son to the next place and carrying me to the next place. And afterward, I could breathe. I could breathe.

Crying is an opening, a cathartic channel for the expression of the soul's deepest complexities. When we cry out of guilt, pain, remorse, joy, self-pity, forgiveness, anger, desperation, loneliness—we are not standing outside of suffering, but giving birth through it. We are present and attending to the complex richness that presents itself from the darkest parts of our feeling selves. We are no longer frozen or sleeping—we are conscious. And through that consciousness the grip of stories that simply no longer serve us can be identified and eventually dissipate, leaving the air clearer than before. Defenses are stripped, and what remains is the awareness of pure love and humility. Clear sight.

Vinny

I paused, leaning on the shovel for a moment. I still couldn't believe what had happened. I had been running in the woods with our boxer, Maia, and we had come to a road crossing. I held on to her collar, and as I leaned over, the ear bud fell out of my ear. I went to grab it, and Maia thought I was giving her the signal to go. She bolted out with faith in me and was immediately struck by a car. She wasn't killed, but her abdomen was split completely open, and I could see her intestines and other organs. I picked her up and ran to my truck. She was gasping. I kept telling her to hold on. I called for my sister, and the two of us got a hold of our mother, who told us to meet her at the vet on West River Street. There was a lot of blood, and Maia wasn't doing so well. She was rasping and trying hard to get a breath. And the vet was closed. It was 5:30. We called the number, and the recording told us we needed to go all the way to South Reno (which is about 45 minutes away). Maia wouldn't make it that far. My sister, mother and I each touched the dog and my mother said very quietly, "It's OK Maia, you can go. You've been a good dog, and we love you. It's OK to go." And she went. She got very still. And it was so damn sad.

I was replaying this scene in my mind as I was digging her grave in the rocky soil on our property. My head was spinning with anguish. "How could I have been so stupid?" "How could I have hurt this beautiful dog?" It was all my fault. Then my girl-friend, mom and I started remembering Maia—how she used to sleep with the cat, and all we went through with her anxiety until she got her own dog door. She was a loyal, beautiful, and kind creature. And the more I talked and cried, the more I felt this opening in my chest near my heart. It was like in the midst of this terrible, terrible suffering and loss, there was this ray of joy. And the more I cried the bigger the joy got. I couldn't believe I could feel both of these things at once. In the place of my darkest pain there was happiness.

It is out of this blessed love—the tears that Kai and Gerda cry in compassion—that they earn their freedom. The pieces of ice that formerly made up the "mirror of reason" begin to dance. The message here is that you must surrender to the larger force of love to understand the presence of "eternity," which is a state of ultimate connection. Wendell's story of coming "out of the abyss" illustrates this sensitivity well.

Wendell[6]

My name's Wendell Mandanay, and though I've lived in this neighborhood for nearly 70 years, most folks know me as the

---

[6] Mark Blickley, "The Pigeon Man Sings," in *Inside Grief,* ed. Line Wise (In-cline Village: Wise Press, 2001), 56-59. Excerpted by permission of Wise Press.

Pigeon Man. Kids sometimes taunt me. They shout, "Pigeon Man! Pigeon Man!" like it is something I should be ashamed of. But I don't really think they mean any harm. They're just bored, that's all, though I do get upset when they throw stones at the birds.

I've been feeding pigeons for 18 years. I try not to miss a day. Sometimes my shoulder acts up, starts really hurting, and it's too painful to even put my coat on. That's when the pigeons miss a meal. Those kinds of days seem to be more frequent lately, and I feel bad for the birds.

I still can't believe that I, Wendell Mandanay, 12 years older than my wife, Anna, would outlive her by 18 years. Do you know that after dozens of years of living with that woman, the thing I miss most about her is her smile?

The day after I buried my wife, I stopped eating. I didn't plan to stop feeding myself; it just happened. I enjoyed the taste of certain foods and had earned considerable praise for my cooking skills, but now the only taste I desired was beer. And plenty of it. All I had to do was pick up the phone, and 30 minutes later there'd be a case outside my door.

When Anna was alive, we enjoyed taking walks and entertaining in our home. But these days I kept close company with the television set. I'd spend most of the time lying on the couch, sipping beer and listening to the TV. The television talked at me day and night. Sometimes I'd awaken in the morning or the afternoon or at night and to my surprise recall the exact content of programs overheard in my sleep.

The neighbors grew concerned. Every couple of days it seemed someone would knock on my door. I'd rouse myself from the couch, place the beer bottles on the floor beneath the coffee table and quietly answer the door.

"Good afternoon, Wendell."

"It's a fine afternoon."

"How are things going, Wendell?"

"I'd say about 360 degrees."

"Is there anything I can get you, Wendell?"

"As a matter of fact, there is."

"What is it, Wendell? What do you need?"

"I could use a smile. Whenever I answer a knock, I never see one. Everybody always looks so upset, so nervous."

"That's because we're worried about you, Wendell."

"But it's all the unhappy faces at my door that make me worry."

"If I can be of assistance, Wendell, you know where to find me."

"Thank you. But to find you would mean that I lost you, and I hope our friendship never comes to that. Good afternoon."

I just wanted to be left alone. When Anna died, not only did I lose my appetite, but I stopped cleaning our apartment. And then I stopped cleaning myself.

About a month or so after my wife's funeral, I was watching a nature show on public television. It was about pigeons. I was asleep, a little groggy, and didn't pay much attention. Not too much sunk in, or so I thought.

When I woke up the next morning (or a few hours later) and went to the fridge for a beer, I kept hearing the narrator's voice in my head. He was telling me things like:

"Pigeons usually mate for life, rearing squabs season after season, often for 10 years or longer."

"All pigeons naturally love to bathe and keep their feathers clean and shining."

"Pigeons do not overeat."

"Mated pigeons are generally more productive if the male is decidedly older than the female."

I thought it was strange remembering that program because I always hated pigeons. To me they were nothing more than flying rats. And let me tell you, they made my life miserable when I was a mailman.

I quickly forgot about the birds when I discovered that I was down to my last three bottles of beer. When I phoned the corner liquor store, they refused to deliver. I owed them money from the last bill.

This meant I had to go out to get it. And going outside was the last thing I wanted to do. I didn't want to get cleaned and dressed, yet I didn't want people to see me like that. So I compromised by taking a shave and hiding the rest of myself under a hat and overcoat Anna had dry-cleaned for me. It was still in its plastic bag.

After pouring two bottles of beer down my throat, I closed the door behind me. On the way to the liquor store I saw a huge flock of pigeons. Some wretch had dumped bags of garbage in front of my building, and the birds were having a feast.

They were all gobbling up that garbage except for this one bird. He had his back to the food and looked as if he was tucked real tight inside his feathers. I walked around to face him.

I wasn't in front of him more than two seconds when he lifted his beak and stared up at my face. I got such a chill looking at his eyes, and this was in the middle of August. I tried to walk away but couldn't. The pigeon wouldn't let me go.

That's when I realize the bird wasn't eating because he'd lost his mate. So I kneeled down, a bit unsteady from the beer I'd just drunk and the heavy overcoat, and gave him a pep talk. I told him to stop feeling sorry for himself, to stop punishing himself because his wife would hate to see him like that. I whispered that his wife had a husband she could respect and it was unfair to her memory if he became a bird that couldn't be respected.

And don't you know, the pigeon starts bobbing his head as if he's agreeing with me. So I stood up and hurried over to the grocery store for some birdseed. When I returned, he was gone. The other birds were still pecking at the garbage, but my pigeon had disappeared.

Being out in the fresh air must've made me hungry. That night I cooked myself a big supper. The next day I began to feed the pigeons, just in case my bird was part of a hungry flock.

Some people are well versed in building a relationship with things that cannot be seen or touched or understood logically. Others, particularly those who feel stuck in the Abyss, may need some more concrete strategies. Chapter Six offers the power of symbol-making as one avenue to building a bridge with the intangible void that death so often presents.

"Though the gravesite would seem to be a place where we let go of the dead, it is also the place where we greet them again as angels."[1]

Greg Mogenson

6

Singing Over Bones

In the Tlingit tale, the pivotal moment occurs in the story when "the image seemed to groan from its chest, like wood groaning, and the Chief realized that the statue was unwell. He asked someone to help him move the statue from where it had customarily stood, and there in the house, beneath the statue and on top of the floor, grew a small red cedar tree." Nyctea recreates the lost bird to the best of her memory. As she undertakes this task, "She sings softly, like a grandmother would to a child. And through the breath going in and out, in and out, which creates the rhythm of her song, she warms the clay, which slowly gives way to flesh, and feather, and heartbeat. And when her song is finished, the owl opens its yellow/green eyes, spreads its wings and flies." The transition from being in the Abyss to facilitating a creative outcome to mourning is reflected in these gestures. And as Nyctea models, it is best done in a place of

---

[1] Greg Mogenson, *Greeting the Angels* (Amityville: Baywood, 1992), xi.

unconditional love. In *moving* the statue and *singing over the bones* the living are assisting the dead in their development. In turn, we are helping ourselves.

A true story from John Muir's[2] life shows the themes of being stuck in the abyss and the pivotal moment when he is called back to life and love.

John's father was a stern and critical Scot, who was very hard on his son. One summer, he asked John to dig a well on the family farm. Every day John would dutifully be lowered in a bucket down to the bottom of the very narrow hole and put soil in the bucket. One of the farm hands would pulley it up. Day after day he would do this, even though he didn't like it and the well became quite deep. Around 75 feet down, he didn't know what was wrong, but he started feeling woozy. It seems there were some noxious fumes that were seeping into the space, but he was unaware of how poisonous they were. Still, every day he would consent to be lowered into that space, and try with all his might to dig. One day, when the fumes were really bad, he felt like sitting down in the bottom of the hole, so he did. He became dizzier and more clouded in his thinking and realized that he couldn't move. He tried a few times, but his limbs quite simply didn't respond. He was numb in his mind and in his body. And after some time, he thought, "It's OK, it doesn't matter," and he gave in to giving up.

---

[2] John Muir, *unpublished lecture* by Laird Blackwell, Ph.D. in Ego, Unconscious, and Search for Soul at Sierra Nevada College, Incline Village, NV (March, 1986).

As he drifted in and out of consciousness, looking up the narrow passageway to the light, he caught a glimpse of a tree branch shimmering as it caught the sun. And there was something in that image that spoke to him, called him toward the light and towards life. It was beautiful and it was moving and it was ALIVE.

And he said to himself, "John, get in the bucket." But alas, he could not move. "Get in the bucket!" Inch by excruciating inch he lifted his arm and put it in, and then one leg, and a torso, until at last his whole body was in the bucket and he was eventually lifted to safety. Soon thereafter, he decided the farm life was not for him, and he followed his instincts and headed west where he discovered his soul home in his beloved Yosemite Valley.

The parallels to being stuck in, or possessed by, the stories we tell ourselves about grief are many. At the bottom of the well is where the life-sustaining essence, water, is found. But often times, we are unaware of the danger of the noxious fumes that may be soundlessly seeping in all around us. These intangible complexes, like those discussed in the previous chapter, weave their way into our psyches like mistletoe on a cedar and insulate us from our keen sense of knowing and reacting. We become numb and cut off. We become delusional ("It's not so bad"). And then, quite unconsciously we choose to psychologically die (or crawl into the casket with our beloved). It is important to identify those stories or behaviors that don't support love (those noxious fumes), so we can set ourselves up for a shift in perspective.

Diane

My husband shot himself in the heart after he learned that I was having an affair. I can't describe the amount of guilt I feel. But after some time it occurred to me, "I didn't pull that trigger. He pulled the trigger." Though I feel terrible, I didn't make that decision, he did. I went from feeling utter embarrassment to feeling profoundly humbled. We live in a world where things happen and I don't know his destiny. I really don't. This realization helped me move toward being able to forgive myself. Notice that I did not say that I will forget. I will never forget. The experience still wrenches through me, but at least it is moving and not stagnant in the pit of my stomach anymore.

Ann[3]

Our story is one of two desperate and ordinary people—desperate because we were losing hope for ourselves, and ordinary because what was happening to us goes on every day in the lives of countless people just like us. It is also a story of the Numiniosum, or presence of the divine spirit.

When Bob and I married, the vows included the phrase, "With my body I thee worship." It went like this: "With this ring I thee wed, with my body I thee worship. With all that I am, and all that I have, I honor you, in the Name of the Father, and of the Son, and of the Holy Spirit." Including that phrase was just

---

[3] Ann Hedge-Carruthers, unpublished manuscript. Reprinted by permission.

the kind of thing that two smart-alecky, overly-educated people would do. I don't know whose idea it was initially. It might have been mine. But we were both pleased with the idea. "With this body I thee worship" came from one of the most ancient Prayer Books in the Anglican tradition and we had knowingly taken it completely out of context. In that era it had meant that a man was designating this woman to be his wife, not his concubine. But Bob and I were doing it for entirely different reasons. We had discovered in one another an excitement and creativity in our sexuality that neither had known before. We wanted to celebrate it.

When a loved one is diagnosed with dementia, the first thing a spouse or child tries to do is keep the one they love looking presentable to the world. But they eventually fail. Later, there is the struggle to keep them looking presentable to friends who stop by. There too, they fail. In the end, the struggle is to keep the loved one presentable to themselves. The latter, with time, becomes as impossible as the former two. People with dementia fail and falter, and as they do they become more horrified by themselves. Bob said to me one day, I am going mad and I must not take you with me.

As the years passed, Bob had less and less control of himself and certainly of life. The mechanisms that had readily gotten food to his mouth or brushed his teeth grew slack along with everything else. One terrible day, Bob stood over me leaning heavily on his walker as I, on hands and knees, cleaned the bathroom floor after he had missed the commode. He said in the most grieved voice, a voice choked and laden with sadness, that came from the deepest parts of his soul, "Annie, my princess." Then he paused, as he tried to find his voice and started again,

"My princess, I never in all my life intended that that you should have to be doing something like this—never—never."

I am not sure what I was thinking in the moment just before he spoke. When a loved one is ill, every day brings something new that one must do for them. I was living life for two people. Whatever I did for myself, I did for him. Two meals to be eaten. Two baths to be taken. Two heads to be combed. Two. Two. Two. Two. I would find myself caught between fatigue and mindless, rote behaviors. I am quite sure that at times I showed little emotion—just blunted responses and reactions. And I dared not think of what the next day might hold for us.

It is said that dementia destroys souls, and if this is true, it is and not just the soul of the one diagnosed as afflicted. Bob had feared that he would take me into madness with him and his fear had not been entirely unfounded. But when I heard him speak that day, I was completely taken out of that self-involved place. The pain in his voice was not a pain that I could have ignored had I tried. Nor could I have let his concern for me go unheard. In that split second I was standing with Bob before friends and family on our wedding night. We were on a balcony looking out over the canyon as the sun set; Bob, so handsome in his linen jacket. I heard the vow that I had made decades before and then had almost entirely forgotten. It had struck me now with a fresh and powerful meaning. I stopped what I was doing, looked up at Bob and said with a strong, clear voice that came from some-where deep inside, "Bobby, with my body, I thee worship."

Everything shifted in that moment. The most beatific smile came over Bob's face; he remembered! Disease had not robbed him of that memory. Those words made our circumstances as close to OK for him as it possibly could be. For that moment, his shame was gone. For me, I received a renewed sense of purpose and courage—that second wind that runners talk about.

That day, by God's mercy, I found the truth in the claim that we can stand almost anything, perhaps all things, if we can find meaning in them. Tending to Bob had now taken on a sacramental quality. That vow and the remembrance of it, carried both of us through to the end. I can truthfully say that I loved him more the day he died than I had in the most passionate days of our romance. I have been blessed.

Kathie

After much indecision, I decided to attend the sentencing for the young man who was driving when my son was killed. Like my mother's death, it was an alcohol-related accident. I walked to where he was seated, in handcuffs, and I hugged him and told him, "I want you to come out of this whole." He said he would and he was thankful for the support. I cried, he cried. I hugged him again before he left the courtroom. I realized at some point earlier in the morning that I needed to display my support, my encouragement, my love, and to do that, my action was going to be required. I kept hearing something in my mind, something I read shortly after Dan passed: "Don't let me die while I am still alive." I was also thinking about the various opinions, even scrutiny I've felt as to my perspective on life after my son, Dan's passing. The driver, Kelley, was Dan's friend, his buddy, someone he loved. This was Dan's path. It certainly wasn't what I wanted, nor ever imagined, but here we are. My family, his family, our family of friends, all our lives were changed that early morning in March. After the hearing one of my deputies came to talk with me and shared that others have commented on how strong I am. I don't know about that. What I do know is this: Love is a choice, and it is also a verb. When offered, I know that love wins every time. My other son, Nick, demonstrates this grace every single day and educates me through his actions. Each of us has opportunities to be kind and demonstrate compassion, to be the hands and feet of God, and those opportunities in and of themselves present us with a tremendous transformative gift. Now that's a package I want to open again and again. I want to and so I choose to live an expansive life filled with compassion, grace, and love. It's a choice available for each of us.

Forgiveness for oneself and others is a way of changing a toxic story. It is a state of ultimate grace, but it can be confusing as a construct. To be clear, it is not saying, "I don't hurt." It is not saying, "I will forget." It is not saying, "What happened is OK." It is usually, quite simply, a change in the way we see things. Sometimes we can open our perspective on our own, and other times, we need some help. It is very difficult business. To consider forgiveness is to enter into the very heart of the pain, to sit with the tension of this discomfort, and choose to re-envision who we are in relation to it.

Dom

I am a 71-year-old man who had been waiting very patiently for the right love. It seemed that everyone had some idea of who

I should be with, and I went on painful date after painful date. Finally, I met her. Consuelo was sparkling, bright, funny, and beautiful. She made me want to be a better man from the moment I saw her. We talked and we danced and we filled in the missing pieces in each other's puzzles. I felt as if I had come home. We only had four months on this earth together before God took her, sadly on the night that I was going to ask her to be my wife. It was a stabbing pain, and I knew the anger of a life so unfair, and I shouted to God that I hated him. In one of my worst moments, it felt as if my heart was literally breaking. As I held my chest, I looked up. An enormous, buckeye butterfly with these beautiful yellow and black circles, bright blue dot in the middle, came to rest on a lodgepole pine right next to me. It flapped its wings flirtatiously and slowly drew me into its beauty. As I leaned forward to take a closer look, the eyelike circles seemed to look right into my soul, and the pain in my chest went away. And then it flew away. And it took my breath away, this beauty. And I thought, "That's my Consuelo. A beautiful butterfly who landed near me. How lucky could a man possibly be? And she is a butterfly, and butterflies must move on." Something changed for me right then. I didn't take it personally and I didn't blame God. I just felt grateful.

Some need to consciously attend to factors that keep one "stuck in the abyss." For others, this shift takes place quite naturally. It is important to notice that a byproduct of this movement is often the re-emergence of creativity. In Greek mythology, it is interesting that Mnemosyne, which means "memory," is the mother of the nine Muses, who are thought to be the inspiration for literature, science, and the arts. The Muses are creativity personified, and they have been birthed by "Memory." The idea is that once we use our memories and imaginations to instigate the shift of perspective, we find that fresh images and new understandings break through. And those images tend to be unique reflections of the individual relationship we have with the deceased. Like John Muir, every person has a tree branch—that thing that shimmers and calls us back to life and love. If we are paying attention, the remarkable thing is that it is the deceased themselves who often offer us the metaphors that we need to survive and stay in connection. Add the ancient folktales, which have set out the trail markers for us, and we need only to be receptive to begin to know the way.

Like Nyctea, you have gathered the bones, or re-created the image of your lost loved one. You have been to the bottom, stripped of all your navigational tools and experienced the most frightening parts of yourself. You have cried and felt stuck in your own despair. But as with all stories, things do not stay static. Nyctea, in a place of sacred communion with the dead, sings the bird a new life. In the Tlingit story, the Chief becomes sensitive to the deceased's desire for movement. It is significant that he is deeply in grief and sitting beside, or attending to, the image of his wife. It is in this state of profound connection that he becomes aware of the need for the deceased to be free. The image becomes "unwell" if not allowed to move. In facilitating her movement, the Chief simultaneously and unknowingly *gives himself permission to move*. As Mogenson says, "We shift our attention from ourselves to them, [and] the awareness begins to dawn that they have a destiny beyond our tears."[4] Instead of a "statue," which is a frozen amalgamation of the image of the deceased, there is something new—a young, red cedar sapling, or a symbol of that which has been co-created out of what lies between the living and the dead. Instead of an inanimate, static replica of the owl, Nyctea uses her wisdom and love to breathe new life into it. Fresh images are creatively emerging.

Signs indicating that movement is imminent are different for each person and may be more subtle. It is perhaps a whisper in the background, which isn't really a voice, but sound and light. It may be in the flicker of a votive candle or the sparkle on a craggy, granite slope. You may suddenly notice, as you are sitting somewhere, that unexpectedly the music sounds particularly rich. Or, that the smell of the vegetables roasting feels warmly soothing. Maybe you have an important dream with a life-changing message from the deceased.

Other people may become aware of this shift more concretely. You decide to color your hair or agree to meet a friend for a long walk. If you are the Pigeon Man, you give a pep talk to a bird. The woman from Chicago begins collecting discarded, single gloves. The Truckee woman sets up car seat checkpoints. The little girl who lost her mother has tea every Sunday and sets a place at the table for her mom. You feel pulled to become involved in something that has meaning for you. The concrete slab of depression begins to crack, and there are tiny, fragile forms of life emerging. The path materializes in front of you. This new growth is being watered with the saltwater truth of tears and Lady Death's second cup, one small sip at a time.

---

[4] Mogenson, *Greeting the Angels*, 31.

In a version of "Cinderella," that I heard in a clearing next to a creek at Sugar Pine Park, the story begins:

In olden times when people still believed in the magic of animals, there lived a man, his wife, and their beloved daughter. One year, when the days became shorter the wife took to her bed, her gaze as heavy as trees under the first snow. And even though there were blood red beets and white parsnips in the bin and an ample fire in the hearth, a blackness hung over the home—you see, Death was sitting softly in the corner of the room. The wife called to her pious daughter and whispered, "Be good and kind, my beloved, and I will be with you always. I am the voice beneath the beat of your heart. If you are very still you will hear me." With that her breath became raspy and labored and Death rose to take her by the arm.

The maiden grieved greatly, and while the ash trees remained frozen in stillness, she visited the lonely headstone on the hill every day. As she wept, she would try to still her thoughts, listening for her mother's voice. Thrice daily, she would prayerfully attend to her good mother's grave, and the cold times passed this way. By the time the crocuses and daffodils pushed through the melting snow, the man had taken another wife, who brought two daughters with her. And even though their faces were lovely, there was something of a vile snake beneath their smiles which the man could not see.

As soon as the man went on a long trip for business, the three women revealed their true nature. They taunted the maiden and made her scrub the clothing, cook the meals, and carry all the firewood. Dark circles deepened under her eyes and her hands became reddened and chaffed from the labor. She was reduced to wearing rags, and sleeping on the smooth stones next to the dusty fireplace. Because she was always covered with ash and filth, they came to call her "Cinderella." Though her body strained like an oxen under the weight of the plow, and her rest was fitful, she held the blessing of her mother close to her bosom. The maiden's spirit remained true and kind.

When the strawberries became plump with juice, and the calves were almost as big as their mothers, the man sent a messenger to his house. The messenger relayed that the man was at a grand festival and was asking what the girls would like him to bring back. "Pretty dresses," clapped the step-sisters, "shiny things for our hair." When it was the maiden's turn, she said, "Tell him to collect the first willow branch that his horse tramples, and bring it back to me." When the man returned, he gave the step-sisters their gifts, and to Cinderella, the frayed end of a willow shoot.

Cinderella planted the willow shoot near her mother's grave on the top of the hill. As she was mounding up the soft, black earth around the base, she cried the tears of a young woman who has known great pain. And thrice daily, she watered the little shoot with her faithful and generous weeping. By the time the fields were furrowed for the next planting, the shoot had grown into a fine-looking little tree. And it was in this weeping willow, that a little, white turtle-dove built her nest. If Cinderella was quiet in herself, and listening to the sound beneath the beat of her heart, she could ask the bird for a wish. And the turtle-dove would give her what she desired.

--◈--

This tale serves as a powerful enactment of the importance of an imaginal relationship with the deceased and describes how that relationship sets the stage for a creative outcome. The story begins with the loss of the *good* mother. Like the husband and wife in the Finnish folk tale, it is the end of the peaceful and harmonious state of their marital bliss that, in turn, lays the foundation for the ensuing challenges and growth. The death of Cinderella's mother may be seen as her initiation into a new state of affairs or a departure from that which is emotionally familiar. The task is to let that which no longer can sustain her, in this case her mother's physical presence, truly die. In her grief, Cinderella forges a different relationship with her mother. Through paying homage three times a day to her memory, she can be seen as having created a space and a place for respect. Both the living and the dead are receiving validation.

It is from the mutually interdependent state that Cinderella *and* her mother are allowed to develop further in the story. The acquisition and planting of the sprig of willow signifies this new growth. The dismembered shoot, which has been separated from that which supported it before, is now ready to take on a new, autonomous form and grows into a tree. It is ready to serve as a living symbol of development—both Cinderella's and her mother's. Significantly, it is watered by tears.

The work of grief, for all these folkloristic figures, results in expansion. For Cinderella, it is her mindful attendance to her mother that results in the growth of the willow tree. For John Muir, his suffering in the hole is relieved by an invitation from a shimmering branch. For the Chief, the movement of his sorrow is symbolized by the emergence of the red cedar tree that has been watered by his tears. It is interesting that modern memorial practices often include the planting of trees. We may not know that we are tapping into an ancient and mythic belief system, but we are.

In myths and stories throughout the world, the tree is a particularly charged symbol which holds both personal and collective meanings. In some traditions, it is seen as an integration of the masculine and feminine because it draws its energy from deep within soul-mother-earth and spreads its branches upward, attracting energy from spirit-father-sky. It is out of this co-creation that all new life is born.

The tree is also believed to be a bridge between the material and spiritual worlds. In Norse mythology, the Yggdrasi is considered the Great World Tree that links and supports the universe. The sky is said to rest on its branches, and it provides a connection between this world and the others. In Judaism, the Kabbalistic Tree,[5] which is sometimes called "the ladder of lights," represents many levels of the tangible and intangible that connect the material and divine worlds. The top is the formless point from which something is created out of nothing, the spirit world. The roots are material reality. The support structures in between represent the energies of expansion, contraction, and equilibrium. The trunk itself is the "Pillar of Consciousness" and is the means by which one brings balance to all the energies—a reminder that each person as an incarnate being who is infused with spirit and returns to the divine, but has the powerful capacity of intent in the in-between places.

In other parts of the world, Indian lore tells of Parizataco's daughter, who killed herself because she had fallen in love with

---

[5] Ami Ronnberg, Kathleen Martin eds., "Kabbalistic Tree," *The Book of Symbols* (San Francisco: Taschen, 2012): 142.

the sun, which did not reciprocate her affection. It is said that the Tree of Sorrow, a Night Jasmine, grew from her grave. This beautifully fragrant flower only opens at night, thus avoiding the burning exposure to her lost lover, the sun. In Native American tales, such as the Tlingit story, trees are believed to house the animate spirits of supernatural beings, including the deceased. Similarly, the Druids believed that trees housed ancestors and the most sacred of trees, the oak, was "daur" in Celtic, which is the foundation of the modern word for "door." Thus doors were seen as a connection between the world of the living and that of the dead. Worldwide, the tree is closely associated with birth and regeneration, life and death, and the tension between these places. It makes sense that they would appear in both folktales and modern rituals to honor the deceased.

In the Tlingit tale, it is also important that the tree that is co-created out of the loving connection is a red cedar. In the symbolism of alchemy, discussed earlier, red is one component in the cycle of white (life) and black (death), and signifies the integration of these two states. It is the color of creation. And cedar is a wood that preserves things. It is strong and fragrant, and repels predatory insects. Thus, "red" and "cedar" together conjure up the image of a protective vessel for the rhythms of life and death. But significantly, it *grows*.

The facilitation of this growth into a new state of being, for the living and the deceased, requires several things: a surrender to Lady Death (an awareness of the cycle of life-death-life); patience; the ability to see yourself compassionately, directly experiencing the shadow sides of yourself; the expression of anger and pain; reimagining yourself in relation to the deceased; and faith in the fact that *love is more powerful than death*. It is in this state that one can invite or generate the particular symbols that will create a bridge between you and your lost loved one.

Symbol-making

Though our loved ones lose their physical reality, they gain a psychological one, changed by death. And this psychic reality is as much a product of the bereaved's unconscious as it is a representation of the deceased person, and when manifested as a symbol, it can be invested with both personal and collective power. Thus the symbol or ritual is created out of that which lies *between* the dead and living. Mourning is an active, creative process. Mogenson says: "Like photographs in the family album, the images of the dead populate the soul. The mourning process is the laboratory in which the images life has imposed upon the film of death are developed."[6]

Whether or not one believes in life after death, the dead are alive in our imaginations, memories, dreams, visions, in how we act and who we are. They are psychologically present. Our job is to help the deceased by giving them a form and means of expression through our own imaginations. In doing so, we help ourselves. We are staying in relationship.

Albert

My way of loving my son is that I take care of his grave year-round. In the summer, I make sure the grass is fertilized and that there are always live flowers. I clean and polish the head-

---

[6] Mogenson, *Greeting the Angels*, 24.

stone and make sure everything is trimmed. I like doing the work and I talk to him while I am doing it. He doesn't "answer back" out loud or anything, but I know what he is saying in response. And it's funny because I used to think I just knew him so well that I would know what he would say. But sometimes he surprises me, and we have conversations about new things that he would never have known about. And he helps me through things. I don't know if that makes me crazy, but I really like my time in the cemetery with Michael. In the winter, I clear out the snow on the ground over his casket, and in some winters, we get quite a bit of snow, so it is a lot of work. But I don't mind. About five years ago, I was helping with some clean up down by the river after a storm, and there were twigs and branches everywhere. I saved a bundle and went to see Michael. For some reason it occurred to me to sit down next to him, and I started putting the twigs in the snow in an upright pattern around his area. I enjoyed doing it, and I left them there through the winter. In the spring when the snow started melting, I noticed that there were little leaves coming out of some of the twigs. They were ALIVE. When the snow was too melted to hold them up anymore, I went back to the river and planted all the sprigs on the banks to help prevent erosion. And some of them continue to grow, so I have repeated this pattern each year. Michael loved the river, and I know he is smiling. I am doing something good for him.

Cary

My son had an accident while four-wheeling. When my wife and I went to the hospital, he was hardly recognizable. He had tubes and a ventilator and he was hooked up to all kinds of contraptions. But the blipping on the screen told us his heart was beating. It is unreal, this moment when you sit beside someone you desperately want to keep in this world, and you see those grim faces of the nurses and you know that he is slipping away. We were told that there was no activity in his brain and a very nice lady talked to us about organ donation. It was hard to jump from hoping he would stay alive to considering giving away parts of him. Later that day, my wife said, "What about his heart? We can't give away his heart!" We were both a mess. And I was thinking of that first time we heard our baby's heart on the machine when Sarah was pregnant. That's when it all finally felt real to me. I was really going to be a dad.

His heart.

Then I remembered an article I had read about a doctor at Cincinnati Children's Hospital[7] who recorded dying children's heartbeats. He then created musical pieces using the heartbeats. I am a musician, too, and I was very inspired by this idea. I thought it would be a good way to "keep" Travis' heart with us, and it would also give me something to *do*. I really needed something to *do*. We hooked up a stethoscope to a recorder and we got a clear recording of that beautiful sound before we let him go. Right after the memorial, I started working on a song. Travis loved country music, so I started with those patterns as the melody, always using the sound of his heart as the beat. I have made a few different songs in different genres, to match my moods. I listen to them every single day.

---

[7] Brian Schreck, http://www.health24.com/Multimedia/Dying-childs-heart-beat-is-turned-into-music-20140528, retrieved 8/26/15

Peggy

My father loved birds of all sorts. When my sister and I were little, he would drag us out of bed at 4:00 a.m. to go up to Honey Lake to see the dance of the sage hens when they were mating. My mother thought he was crazy. He also took us up to "Chickadee Ridge," where the birds will land right on your hand and eat the sunflower seeds. My sister and I have many pictures of us trying to stand still, all bundled up in our ski jackets and hats, holding our outstretched palms out waiting for the chickadees. We called them "cheeseburger birds" because that's the sound they would make in the spring time. And they did have "little, dirty, birdy feet," as we used to like to sing. After our father died, I wanted to do something special to honor him. I took a ceramics workshop and found myself really drawn to making birds. I started with an owl (our father's favorite) and then made a sage hen, a hawk, and a chickadee. At that time, I had an urn with half of Dad's ashes sitting on the mantel. And I knew that's not where he wanted to be. So when it came time to do the glazing for the pieces I had made, I took a handful of ashes and stirred them into the glazes. I was so scared the birds would blow up in the kiln and I would have wasted those precious ashes. The pieces were fired and came out really well, beautiful actually. I asked my instructor and husband to help me configure the birds on a totem pole. And together we made something SO GORGEOUS. I gave it to my sister, who now lives in our childhood home. She put it in Mom's garden, and Dad's birds with a part of Dad in them are smiling over us, loving us.

✦

Creative acts in honor of the deceased help both the dead and the living. They can connect the abstract with the concrete, as well as serving as a bridge between our instinctual and thinking senses of self. Most importantly, they give us a means through which we can *still love*. Though the previous examples were all from individuals, there are places and spaces where one can participate with others in the singing up of new life.

One collective example of creative outcomes to mourning can be seen at the Memorial Temples of Burning Man.[8] In late August, the Black Rock desert of northern Nevada USA becomes the temporary home for up to 68,000 people who participate in the Burning Man music and art festival. Organized by the guiding principles of inclusion, gifting, decommodification, self-reliance and radical self-expression, the festival draws artists and free thinkers from around the world.[9] The culminating event is the creation and conflagration of a 100-plus-foot wooden replica of a man. On the final evening of the event, a lesser-known and far more sacred part of the festivities includes the construction and subsequent burning of a memorial temple. Hundreds of people adorn the Temple walls with personal messages, symbols, and/or pictures related to their lost

---

[8] A portion of the section appeared in Kimberly Bateman, "Symbol-Making in Bereavement: The Temples at Burning Man" a chapter in Katarzyna Malecka and Rossanna Gibbs (eds.) *And Death Shall Have Dominion: Interdisciplinary Perspectives on Dying, Caregivers, Death, Mourning and the Bereaved* (London: Interdisciplinary.net, 2015)

[9] Webmaster, Burning Man, accessed August 21, 2013, http://www.burning-man.com.

loved ones. Dozens of pairs of army boots are lined up in a spiral, each with a tag indicating the name of the American soldier who had died in Afghanistan. A little girl's braided hair, with the ribbon still on it, hangs from a piece of wood that simply says "AMY" in purple crayon. A wedding dress hangs from a rafter, blowing in the wind, and the note pinned to it says, "I'm sorry you didn't make it to our wedding." One burner who lost her husband in a parasailing accident writes, "I hope that I can go on without you. I fear that I will."

Van de Castle helps us understand the importance of symbol-making. He says, "Symbols can serve to carry messages from the instinctive to the rational parts of the mind, and can also represent lines of development which are striving for future completion and wholeness. Symbols thus can have both a retrospective and a prospective side: retrospective because of their instinctual origin, and prospective because they are process oriented and move in the direction of further development and growth."[10] The symbol, or memento, thus serves as a bridge between past remembrances and future development, allowing interaction in the present tense. They can also present a pathway from the unconscious to the conscious mind. Johnson said, "When we experience the images, we also experience inner parts of ourselves that are clothed in the images."[11] And, in mining our imaginations and becoming active in our gestures toward our deceased loved ones, we assert our continued relationship with them.

---

[10] Robert Van de Castle, *Our Dreaming Mind* (New York: Ballantine, 1994), p. 159.

[11] Robert Johnson, *Inner Work: Using Dreams and Active Imagination for Personal Growth* (San Francisco: Harper, 1986), 25.

The Temple at Burning Man may be seen as a darkroom for the manifestation of these undeveloped images of the deceased. In this way, the potentially chaotic internal state of the bereaved may become more defined and move toward a new order. In the spiral of the boots walking, in the wave of the beribboned braid, the grief is given shape. Thus, symbol-making can be seen as assisting in greater organization of our thoughts and feelings. Additionally, in the act of symbol-making, attention is shifted away from personal pain, and toward the lost loved one. It may allow an opportunity for the bereaved to love once again.

History is replete with examples of lasting symbols created to recognize the dead. The earliest memorial tablets were recovered in Mesopotamia and are dated 1680 BCE. Other notable examples include the Taj Mahal, erected by Mughal emperor Shah Jahan in memory of his wife, the miles of memorial sculptures at the Père Lachaise cemetery in Paris, and the pyramids commemorating Egyptian kings. The AIDs quilt, Vietnam Wall, Holocaust Memorial and 9/11 Museum are other good examples. The construction of these memorials focuses on taking something from the imaginal back to the concrete. The Temples at Burning Man invite this same process through symbol-making, and then add to this sequence the dissolution of that symbol, reinforcing the concept of impermanence, relationship to the abstract, and community. The team that constructed the Temple of Flux noted:

> To lead our design thinking we look to the idea of Counter-Monument. A phrase coined by James Young to define a new way of thinking about memorial/monument: The counter-monument's aim is not to console but to provoke; not to embody

permanence but change; not to be everlasting but to disappear; not to be ignored but to demand interaction; not to accept the burden of memory but to throw it back and demand response. The counter-monument accomplishes what all monuments should; it reflects back to the people and thus codifies their own memorial projections and preoccupations.[12]

In the burning, the image of the deceased may move from one that is concretized and bound by physical time and space to a more fluid image that exists in the imaginal space. There is presence, albeit psychic, where there used to be absence. One view of writing on the Temple walls would be to see the bereaved as becoming an active participant in weaving the past into the present and forging a different type of relationship with the deceased.

It is significant that the dissolution of the memorial symbols that adorn the Temple is accomplished by fire. From an archetypal perspective, fire presents a mesmerizing, but disturbing ambiguity. Fire destroys, as well as fertilizes, as a forest blackened sets up the potential for regrowth. It is a dual image in that one can burn with joy and also burn in complete disintegration.[13] Thus fire holds the opposites of creation and destruction and accurately mirrors the bereaved's relationship to the

---

[12] Temple of Flux team, quoted in Lee Gilmore, "The Temple: Sacred Heart of Black Rock City," http://burningman.org/event/art-performance/playa-art/building-the-temple/, retrieved 8-26-15.
[13] Clarissa Pinkola-Estés, *Women Who Run with the Wolves* (New York: Ballantine, 1995), 228.

deceased. There is the dissolution of a physical relationship juxtaposed with the construction of a psychic or imaginal relationship.

Fire has long been seen as a potent metaphor for a multiplicity of conflicting emotions, including passion, anger, and the life-force itself. The Archive for Research in Archetypal Symbolism points out that historically:

> The Greek Heraclitus imagined a kind of fiery ether as the primary constituent of the cosmos and the soul as composed of a similar fire—as the materials and structures of civilizations have been built and renovated by fire-craft, so is the stuff of the self worked by the libidinal fires of urges, instincts, affects, and desires. Their intensity brings things to the surface, releases and propagates golden seeds, calcinates, sublimates, refines and tortures, hardens and shapes what is overly pliable and melts or evaporates what is rigidly hard.[14]

Thus, fire is a shape-shifter and often associated with transformation. Its ancient relationship to the alchemist, the metallurgist, the shaman, the witch, the ceramist, and the cook among others, all suggest the possibility of metamorphoses. "It is through fire that Nature is changed," wrote Eliade, making it the "basis of the most ancient magic and in its symbolism carrying, even now, our terrors and hopes of transmutation."[15]

---

[14] Ami Ronnberg and Kathleen Martin, eds., *The Book of Symbols: Reflections on Archetypal Images* (San Francisco: Archive for Research in Archetypal Symbolism), 84.

[15] Mircea Eliade, *The Encyclopedia of Religion* (New York: Routledge, 1987), 170.

At Burning Man, the process of creating and burning the memorials in the Temples is being witnessed and shared, allowing an unusual sense of intimacy and connection among its participants. Pike pointed out that:

> Through the physical inscription of memories on the Temple's walls, and in turn through reading the inscriptions of others, participants were able to share, ritualize, and transform private grief into public expression in ways that are generally unavailable to many contemporary Americans.[16]

In a culture where pain and suffering are often repressed and there is the notable absence of extended rituals to process bereavement, the Temple provides a safe space for the expression of the complexity of emotions associated with loss. "Hundreds of strangers sit in mutual respect, often coming outside of their own anguish to assist another," remarked one burner. "You realize, perhaps for the first time, that you are not alone—everyone is missing something or someone."[17] The personal becomes universal, and the recognition of this archetypal reality allows participants to become more empathic with one another, enjoying a deepened level of connectivity.

From a depth psychological perspective, "successful" mourning culminates in a "letting go" of the deceased and recognition of the fact that they will not be returning. This final phase has received numerous labels: Acceptance,[18] Reorganization,[19]

---

[16] Pike quoted in Lee Gilmore, "The Temple: Sacred Heart of Black Rock City."
[17] Rebecca Cobain, email to author, 2 September 2013.
[18] Elisabeth Kübler-Ross, *On Death and Dying* (New York: Macmillan, 1969), 123.
[19] John Bowlby, "Process of Mourning," *International Journal of Psychoanalysis*, 42 (1961): 317-340.

Recovery,[20] and Healing and Renewal.[21] The common theme is that the bereaved is somehow able to rechannel his or her energy into new people, ideas, and projects. Perhaps those who participate in symbol-making are taking this idea to a new level and facilitating a creative outcome that does not require that they relinquish an attachment to the dead. Instead, perhaps the bereaved are managing to continue a relationship with their loved ones in another order of reality, an imaginal or psychic one.

To summarize, the process of creating symbols for the dead gives reflection and validation to the mourner's relationship to lost loved ones. In death, there is a movement from the concrete (loved one in the physical) to the abstract (loved one in the imaginal). The mourner then moves the image of the deceased back to the concrete (creation of a symbol). In the case of the Temples at Burning Man, the bereaved again witness the transition back to the abstract (dissolution by fire), but this time, they are exerting some control over this process. These practices allow us to recognize, contain, release, and yet *stay in relationship*. In this capacity, the symbols and rituals may have a healing effect for the bereaved. That is, they allow the concrete expression of the deceased in the physical realm and offer a chance for the bereaved to usher it into the imaginal space. In replaying this transition, perhaps the mourner can become more comfortable saying *good-bye* in the physical, while simultaneously creating the opportunity to say *hello* in the psychic or imaginal.[22]

---

[20] Colin M. Parkes, *Bereavement: Studies of Grief in Adult Life* (London: Tavistock, 1972), 48.

[21] Catherine M. Sanders, *Grief: The Mourning After: Dealing with Adult Bereavement* (New York: Wiley & Sons, 1989), 30.

[22] Greg Mogenson, *Greeting the Angels*, 18.

"Love is the way messengers from the mystery tell us things."

Rumi

7

Crossing the Owl's Bridge

In the Tlingit tale, the red cedar tree that emerges from the statue of the Chief's wife grows. In its actualization, it is said to give rise to many other red cedar saplings all over the Queen Charlotte Islands. These trees then expansively generate more fertility, showing a glimpse of the essential nature of grief work. Out of what is co-created between the living and the dead, something new and autonomous develops. That something is "beautiful." And, like a child who is the combination of two people's DNA, it takes on a life of its own.

Nyctea, through her mindful and heartfelt song, breathes life into the reconstructed owl, and it opens its eyes, spreads its wings and crosses the Owl's bridge. She teaches that as much as we need our lost loved ones, the deceased need us as well. They want us to create a home for them and give them expression in our imaginations. We attentively remember the dead, and actively assist in ushering them to the next place. In doing so, we position ourselves at the edge of the great mystery and can conceive of both ourselves and our loved ones in a newly evolved form.

A motif of folktales called "the grateful dead" demonstrate this reciprocity between the world of the living and the dead,

163

as well as showing some of the gifts that may result from this interplay. These stories appear throughout Europe, the West Indies, Spanish America, and parts of Asia, and in them there is a turn of events in which those who are assisted in death later return to help the living. It is out of this relationship that a third entity, or something that lies between the living and the dead, is born. One such story is a Japanese folk tale about Abe No Yasuna.[1]

One day, while out in the woods, Abe No Yasuna happens upon a white fox who is trying to outrun a hunting party of noblemen. In a moment of compassion, he hides the white fox in the folds of his garment and saves it from certain death. A year later, he meets and falls in love with a beautiful young woman named Kuzunoha. She has a distant, otherworldly look in her eyes, and Abe No Yasuno's friends claim that she is haunted. But he is engaged by her charm, and deeply in love, so they marry. Later that year, she bears their son, Abe No Seimei. Soon after his birth, Kuzunoha dies unexpectedly, and Abe No Yasuna grieves the most painful of losses. He considers killing himself and their son because of his tremendous angst. Three days later, Kuzunoha appears to Abe No Yasuna in his dream world and shows her true form. She is the fox whom he had saved. Their son grows up to become a legendary poet, magician, and spiritual advisor to the Emperor.

---

[1] Shigeta Shin'ichi, Gaynor Sekimori and 繁田信一, "Abe No Seimei. *Japanese Journal of Religious Studies*,40, 1, (2013): 77-97.

It is interesting that Abe No Seime, the result of a union between a living man and a mythological creature, is a poet, magician, and spiritual advisor. All three of these vocations reflect special powers of perception, resourcefulness, imagination, and expression. In a sense, Abe No Seime represents the ability to weave together wisdom from the material and spiritual worlds in service of a creative end. It is similar to the challenge bereaved people face in grieving.

One example of someone facing this challenge comes from a pediatric intensive care unit in Worchester, MA. The introduction of this book included the story of sitting with Scot in the back of a car on the way to the mortuary to view the body of our brother Chad, who was killed in an avalanche at age 21. Interestingly, on the day he heard of our brother's death, Scot also found out that he was accepted to medical school. Since that fateful day, Scot has become a physician who has chosen to work in the field of pediatric intensive care. Every day, he deals with life-and-death issues in the very young. His struggle with the loss of our brother has been a defining force in his chosen professional calling and helped him to become a more compassionate doctor. He has known great pain and is able to sit with others who are in that place. Chad is not the only ghost who shapes Scot's interpersonal style, though. When he was a second-year resident, one patient in particular helped him to become aware of the power of spiritual "presences."

Scot

Eleven-year-old Emily had recurrent T-cell lymphoma and was admitted as a "last ditch." She smiled broadly through her steroid-chubby face and was appreciative of all we were doing. To ease the anxiety and create connection, I told her a joke every day I knew her.

"Do you know why gorillas have big nostrils?"

"Because they have big fingers." She giggled. We racked her body with one more round of energy-sapping chemicals. We waited and we hoped.

Despite all our treatments, the cancer metastasized to her spine. Morphine dripped. "More jokes," she said through tears.

"How do you catch a unique rabbit?"

"You neak up on him." She tried to smile. We wanted so desperately for her to be well, but I was aware that she was in great pain. She knew that I could see this. The jokes were for her, and for me. We needed to see each other smile.

One day, Emily called me to her bedside and said, "Scot, what is it going to feel like when I die?" I was only a second-year resident, and I searched my medical school repertoire for an answer.

"You can fight, be strong, and hold on," were the words used, particularly with kids. But her look demanded honesty. We both knew she was dying.

I paused to imagine a place I have never been and I hoped the words came out right.

"I think you will probably feel like you are falling deeper and deeper asleep," I said in a slow, serious voice that quivered. "You will find it harder and harder to wake up and see all of us here, but finally you won't be able to wake up. Instead, you will be in your dreams from then on." The words hung in the air for a moment.

"I like my dreams," she said.

A few days later, Emily paged me and wearily whispered, "It's happening." She asked for a joke, as a joke. It was hard for us to smile. She motioned for me to come closer, and as I leaned in, she said, "Scot, you are going to be a really great doctor."

Her belief in me lasted longer than her body. Emily died that night.

Medical school taught me how to help a child live—about medicines, treatment strategies, and chances. But it was 11-year-old Emily who taught me how to help a child die—about humor, and suffering, and the bald, steroid-chubby beauty of the human essence.

The spirit of Emily's beliefs stand beside me every time I tend to a patient in need. Opening up to her guiding presence helps me to see people on the level of "soul" rather than as their diagnoses. In this way, I believe I am serving love, with Emily by my side.

Scot can be viewed as part physician, part magician, part poet, and fully human. These qualities are the result of an integration of the places of life and death. Like Abe No Seime, he has bridged the material and spiritual worlds and knows that a part of having deeply loved and lost is a connection to something much greater than your own personal story. Grief can be seen as an invitation to see and feel the universal as it germinates all around; to know how love generates more love; which re-creates itself in ever-expanding circles, and to imagine how this love becomes the elixir that saves us all. Death, if allowed, is like a spiritual obstetrician, and what is birthed is Love.

Brie

Four years after my son's death, I was driving in an unfamiliar area. I was feeling intense pain that day. I was realizing that I had been so sad for so long, and there was nothing I could do. I began to cry. Trickles of tears gave way to sobs, and soon I was pleading with my deceased son. "What am I supposed to do! You have to help me here!" I could no longer see the road through the blur of my tears and I realized that I was lost. Now I was distraught, and scared, because I was trying to get across three lanes of traffic. Someone beeped at me, and my heart raced. I swerved in front of someone else and skidded out of control, onto the dirt shoulder.

I got out of the car, still sobbing and looked up. Standing before me, approximately 15 feet high, was a statue of the Virgin Mary holding her dead son in her arms. Her face was sad but serene. The Pietà.

The image was vaguely familiar to me because my grandmother used to take me to church when I was a little girl. All at once, I had what I would call an experience of *cosmic stereo*. I knew wholeheartedly that my pain was a pain that had been experienced by thousands of generations of women before me. An invisible line had been cast back through history, and it connected my mother loss to millions of other losses. I also knew that thousands of generations after me would feel the same pain and that the invisible line was being simultaneously cast into the future. The image of Mary and her deceased son connected past, present, and future. Then I looked at Jesus' face, and my understanding shifted even more. He knew the burden of pain as well. In spirit, he had transcended the pain of the flesh and could serve as a model of freedom. The particular gathered me up and showed me a glimpse of the universal. I was at one with the world, and there was such peace.

Jamie

My husband and I were married for 40 years, and in that time we built houses, raised two children, and a created a rich life together with wonderful friends. We loved to sail and hike, and enjoyed our grandchildren immensely. Jim was always the caretaker, managing our finances, the physical structure of our aging house, and making sure our needs were attended to. When he died of a very aggressive sarcoma, I was a boat without a sail, bobbing listlessly in the changing winds, and the joy seemed to go out of my life.

Two years after Jim's death, I hiked up a trail at Homewood. It brought back memories of our children, because we used to ski there when they were little. And I came to this area that was blocked off with a sign that said, "Revegetation Area." Well, it looked pretty revegetated to me, so I ventured over the rope barrier and found myself in a gorgeous field of fully blooming Jacob's ladders flowers. There was something in the sight and the wind and the nostalgia of that place that made me want to sing. So I sang, "We are climbing Jacob's ladder" at the top of my lungs. I was filled with joy and also with a loving presence. Jim's spirit was there, assuring me, letting me know that he was OK and I was going to be OK. It was a visitation and such a divine gift. When I got home, I looked up the symbol of "Jacob's ladder." I was amazed. In the Hebrew tradition it is a stairway to heaven. It was all at once a flower, a song, a connection to my husband and a relationship to Scripture, beliefs, and traditions that are thousands of years old. It was the many contained in the one and it was all linked by love. Pure love.

Terra

The night my dear friend Elisabeth died, she had become very agitated right before her passing. She sat straight up in bed and said, "I am going on a trip ... I need to pack .... I have things to do ... I am leaving." There was a great deal of urgency before she slipped into unconsciousness and stopped breathing. I lay down next to her for quite some time until the mortuary people came, and I talked to her. I told her I hoped she was with Amah (her grandmother) and Liz (her close friend), Jasper, Marley, and Lucius (her favorite cats). I told her I hoped it was ALL LOVE and colors and music where she was going.

That night I had a dream. In it I said, "Please help me understand death. It is so confusing to me." Elisabeth showed me a very large room. The whole room was an enormous and sophisticated 3-D printer, even though I have never seen one in real life. In the center, a large origami crane materialized with a single, perfect pearl in the middle. The paper was extraordinary.

It was homemade and soft and white. I moved toward it to touch it. As I approached, the individual molecules began dancing and vibrating. I could see threads of charged energy swirling, and there was nothing material to touch. The vibrations collated, and the whole structure FLATTENED. And that was the word Elisabeth used, "FLATTENED." She showed me how the flattened energy then returns through the machine, to be re-constellated elsewhere. I wondered where and if it was in the same form. She gave no answer.

The physical sciences teach us about protons, neutrons, and electrons. These energies cannot be directly observed, but we believe they exist because of the resulting physical manifestations of their dynamics. Through physics, we know that energy cannot be destroyed but simply changes. Similarly, mathematical concepts like the idea of infinity cannot be touched as realities, and yet we accept them as truth. The dream I had about my lost friend feels real to me on both a personal and a scientific level. Everything is made of intangible energy. We are all vibrating force fields. It is a beautiful conceptualization of the continuation of my dear friend in another place and brought me great comfort. It was as if my understanding fit smoothly and neatly into the greater understandings taught to us through science. Elisabeth, the universe, and I are all governed by the same properties, and I like that.

Maria

When I was little, I had an imaginary friend named Bic. He looked a little bit like Casper the Friendly Ghost, and no one else could see him except me. I learned not to mention him to anyone as they would say he wasn't real. I knew they were wrong. When we went on trips he was not allowed to go, so I would find pay phones and sit and talk to him. You know, just fill him in on things he was missing and remind myself that I had a friend. Mostly he helped me to not feel so alone. Bic stayed by my side until I was about nine and he understood everything about me. More importantly, he still liked me. Bic came around less and less as I developed friends at school. I don't remember the last time I saw him, but my parents were relieved that their child was no longer talking to someone they couldn't see. I wasn't afraid, because I knew if I called him he would come back. When he wasn't visible, he lived inside a teddy bear I had named "Rough-n-tough." That teddy bear sat on my bed all the way through graduate school. I am now fifty years old and spent the last year of my life helping a dear friend through a lethal cancer. I watched her undergo treatment after debilitating treatment as they cut pieces of her body out and subjected her to toxic chemicals. She died early last summer and I was able to be with her for a while before the mortuary people came to get her. While I was talking to her, the room took on a reddish glow in the hour after her death. There was something about that color, that warmth that felt like the essence of my friend. A few weeks after her death, a maple tree in our yard turned crimson in the middle of summer. A rose bush in her mother's garden which was formerly white, also made a striking transition to red. And several times, when I was walking on the east end of Donner Lake in the softness of the sunset, the ground and all the lichen took on an other-worldly, red hue. I felt her there. Feeling my friend in the imaginary is a lot like knowing Bic as a child. When I open to her presence, I don't feel so alone. I feel understood. And I feel liked. And to say it is not "real" just isn't true. It is another order of reality. Sometimes I think to myself, "it's all in my imagination." But then I also think, "of course the dead would use our imaginations, what else have they got?"

⬥

The path through grief has been forged before, and it is well marked for those who open themselves up to receiving cues from things unseen. In bereavement, we are at first initiated into a new state of affairs by the death of our loved one. In this unfamiliar psychological territory, we first look around us and then look within, to participate in story-making. We are authoring our loved one's story, and our own, in relation to them. We are moving them from the abstract, back to the concrete. We then must become acquainted with the Abyss, and the cyclic nature of reality: life followed by death followed by life. Lady Death helps us to sit with the ugliest, most disenfranchised parts of ourselves and begin letting what no longer sustains us die. Through symbol-making and ritual, we then loosen our hold on the physical and allow ourselves to release the physical back into the abstract, while still retaining a connection. In endeavoring this practice, we are singing up life for our lost loved ones as well as singing our own souls back home.

"Singing over bones," though a metaphoric reference, appears in several guises in our cultural stories. One notable reference is from the Bible. In Ezekiel 37:24, God promises that Israel will be restored in blessing. However, this development seems like a remote possibility in that as a nation, Israel had been divided and dispersed. Its people were said to be like living dead, without hope. God then gives Ezekiel[2] (37:1-14) a vision of a valley of dry bones with directions to speak to them. He is to tell them that God will breathe life into them. Ezekiel obeys, and the bones magically reassemble, become whole in flesh, and are infused with divine breath. They stand up and become a vast army. It is a sign that the nation will be restored both physically and spiritually, and become whole again. Through Ezekiel and the valley of bones, God has sung the nation back to life.

From a very different part of the world, the American Southwest, another tale relays the metaphoric practice of "singing over bones" as a means of soulful restoration. Pinkola Estés tells the story of La Loba (Wolf Woman)[3], who gathers the bones of creatures, and in particular, wolves. She takes these bones back to her cave and reassembles the wolf, thinking as she does this, of the particular song she will sing for it. When the song is revealed to her, she stands over the wolf and sings. The creature, piece by piece is sung into flesh and fur and heartbeat. And when it is whole, it leaps out of her cave and runs down the canyon, transformed into a laughing woman.

To sing is to use our breath to give expression to what lies in the depths of our being in service to that which is in need of restoration. We give our "breath body" to resurrect that which is in danger of being lost. Ezekial's valley of bones turns into a standing army. In the La Loba story, the result is a laughing woman who runs free.

Another folktale, "The Flower," illustrates how divine breath can rejuvenate those in the land of the living, as well as those in the land of the dead.

---

[2] Ezekiel 37: 1-14, King James Version of *The Holy Bible.*
[3] Clarissa Pinkola Estés, *Women Who Run With the Wolves* (New York: Ballantine, 1997), 25-26.

The Flower

When a good child lies on his deathbed, cheeks as pale as wax, and a body as lifeless and brittle as leaves in the fall, tell him about the angel. The old ones know the story about how the angel with iridescent wings will sit quietly by the foot of the bed. When the time is right, the angel will gently gather up the last breath from the depths of the child's body. With tenderness, that angel will carry the child up above the land, where he will be able to visit all the places and people that he loved during his time on earth. Along the way, the angel might gather some flowers so the child has a present to bring to God. The child gets to choose these very special flowers, for it is said that God will select the flower that pleases him the most and breathe life into it again with a divine kiss. The flower and the child will be reborn and live in God's home.

The old ones will also tell of the young girl who tripped on some tangled roots and fell into a deep ravine. When the kindly angel of God visited her, like a dream she rose up above her broken body and out of her pain. As if through glittering glass, she saw fields of wheat and oats sprouting in furrowed black earth, deep forests and even deeper emerald lakes. The angel told the little girl to choose some flowers to bring to God. "Such a difficult choice," she thought as everywhere she looked, it was alive with color. Apple and pear trees seemed to bend with the burden of their pinkened blossoms. Golden Honeysuckles spread across pale green hedgerows. The daisies shone with their happy little faces, begging the game of "he loves me, he loves me not." Dandelions sat patiently waiting for someone to make them into a crown. But, among the snowdrops, crocuses, violets and all the others, the pea blossoms caught her eye. They were dainty and delicate, pink and white and sent out beautiful curling tendrils in all directions. The angel gathered a large handful. "We are ready to go to God," exclaimed the child with hope.

"Not just yet," replied the angel. He guided them down the narrow, darkened lanes of the village to the refuse pile. There, the child saw rats scrambling behind pieces of old shoes, splinters of broken glass, ashes, and mounds of old cloths and sawdust. The angel pointed to something in the mess. It was a root ball covered with mold. Tracing the decaying stem, the child could see an ordinary field flower, a weed really, which was now very much dead and obviously of no use to anyone. "This one we will present to God with the others," said the angel. "But it is so ugly," thought the child. And reading her mind the angel said, "hush now and let me tell you a story."

"Some time ago, a family lived in a hovel on the edges of town. They were so poor that they often had to sift through the ashes of the fire to find bits of gristle to eat and steal potatoes in the night from their neighbor's fields. When the seventh child was born with a deformity, the mother and father mourned greatly, for he was just another mouth to feed and could not be of any use. When he was old enough, they put him in the root cellar with only one small window, and brought him food when they could. He lived there for a long time, and even though his body did not work, his mind was sharp and he was in need of something to love. One day, a kindly old woman brought him a bundle of field flowers and some plum pudding for Christmas. After licking every finger full of the delicious pudding, he put the flowers in the window, hoping they would continue to bloom. But alas, when he woke the

next day they were all dead, and he was very sad. Then, he noticed that one of the flowers had some roots still attached, so he planted it in some of the shavings from the cellar in an old bucket. The crippled boy moved the bucket each hour to make sure the flower got as much slanting sunlight through the little window as it could, and he was certain to water it. Year after year that little field flower returned. It was the boy's greatest treasure and he lived to see its beauty and breathe its generous fragrance. Lying on his deathbed, it was to the beloved flower that he turned when the angel came to take him away. The flower stayed in the root cellar for some time until it too, died and forgotten, was thrown in the rubbish."

The little girl who had fallen into the ravine looked with wide eyes at the angel. "How is it that you have come to know all this," she asked.

"Because," said the angel, "I am the boy with the deformity who lived in the root cellar." The angel smiled a joyous smile and added the field flower to the bouquet of pea blossoms.

When they reached the other world, God encircled the dead child with his love and breathed life into her with a kiss. As soon as he released her, she could feel her own voice rising and hear it being echoed by the singing of angels. Beyond those angels were the echoes of even more angels, spreading out into infinity like ripples on a pond in a beautiful chorus of love and peace. God then took the bouquet to his heart and kissed the poor field flower. Green pulsed through its stem and the yellowed petals became vibrant and soft. It too, felt its voice again. All were singing together, the child and the crippled boy turned angel, the field flower and God, the small and the great, in ever expanding circles. The old ones say it is all true and that is all they know.

In this tale, God "kisses" the deceased child as well as the withered flower, inspiring a renewed voice and a song. There is life-death-life imagery throughout the story, and all is revivified and connected to the universal through the invisible breath. It is also important to point out that "to sing" is not limited to that specific action, it includes all forms of creative expression—dreaming, building, planting, tending, painting, writing, among others. As an example, another means of re-creating the story of loved ones is through dance.

Colin

As part of the "Moving Stories" project, the Motus O Dance Troupe out of Toronto, Canada, has created a program called "Beauty Marks." The Weaver (facilitator) asks a series of questions to the dying person designed to invoke memories and allows the expression of thoughts, feelings, events, and beliefs. The Weaver then gives the person's story an organizational structure—a beginning, middle, and end. Personal experiences shared by the dying person are animated through choreography and performed by the troupe for the participant and their loved ones. This practice engages imagination, helps people craft a narrative of their life story, and stimulates meaning-making for both the participant and their loved ones. In visualizing and embodying the story rather than verbalizing, it becomes more apparent that one person's story contains universal themes. It is a way of situating one's experiences in the greater context of all stories and allowing those who are left another means through which to love.[4]

When we actively and creatively seek to bridge the spaces of life and death, and the material and spiritual worlds, we become more comfortable with the idea of integrating opposites and connecting the personal with the universal. We start realizing that when we feel most alone, we are actually the most connected. It is like the grove of aspen trees in southern Colorado and Utah that, though made up of thousands of individual trees, is actually considered the largest, single, living organism on the planet. One root system connects and nourishes all the trees in a network that spans over hundreds of acres. Looking metaphorically at this grove, we might see loving someone as tending an individual or personal tree. If the tree is cut down, we who know ourselves in relation to that one tree may become sad and disorganized and bereft. When we become more comfortable in the knowledge that our tree was one beloved part of the greater whole, the recognition of this pattern can lead us out of labyrinth of our own psyches and into an awe of the mystery.

Deepak Chopra said, "All love is based on a search for spirit."[5] In a world where it is increasingly difficult to make meaning and we often feel disconnected, it is no wonder that our expe-

---

[4] Colin Funk, conference presentation, *Making Sense of Dying and Death* (Athens: Interdisciplinary.net, 2013).
[5] Deepak Chopra, *The Path to Love* (New York: Random House, 1997), 65.

riences of universality and love often come through those closest to us. When our loved ones cross the threshold into the intangible, we are often left searching for the energy that animated our relationship. That energy, on the personal level, may be described as "soul." It is interesting to note that in most cultures, the roots of the word "soul" are related to something that loosely translates into an "invisible breath-body." The Latin word "anima," or soul, has the same etymological origin as the Greek word "anemos," which means "wind." Similarly, in Arabic wind is "rih," and "ruh" is the "soul."[6] Worldwide, and throughout all of known history, individual people have been conceptualized as being more than a physical body. The suggestion is that soul can be felt, but it cannot be seen. It is a breath body.

In the material realm, physicists speak of force fields, atoms, and black holes as realities that cannot be empirically substantiated but must be inferred. Similarly, in the psychic realm the conceptualization of "soul" and "spirit" are constructs that point to energies that exist but cannot easily be sensed. We personify these souls and access them through our closest relationships, often forgetting that like a signal conducted through a television set, the destruction of the television set does not mean the end of the signal. Invisible breath bodies require a different way of seeing and knowing.

It is important to remember that it takes more than cancer (or pneumonia, or flu, or diabetes, etc.) to kill a mother. "Mother" is an ancient presence who has been there before, is

---

[6] Carl G. Jung, The Psychological Aspects of the Kore. In H. Read, ed., R.F.C. Hull, trans., *The Collected Works* (Princeton: Princeton University Press, 1947/1969), 345.

here now, and will always be. Whether you like it or not, she is in your head and your heart and a guiding force shaping who you are. We must look for her with soft eyes and see her in the bowls of food on the table, in the sounds made by the river after it rains, in the earthy browns that texture the interior of caves. She is the dark soil upturned by the newly plowed field and the sudden tingling we feel when we see the moon reflected on water. When you awaken and your room smells like love, she has visited.

"Father" does not succumb to heart failure (or stroke, or emphysema, etc.). Your personal father's body may, but "Father" is an inexhaustible, timeless energy. You can see him in the yellowed angle of the sun as it comes through the trees on a misty day; or in the sudden protection you feel surrounded by when in danger. He illuminates the North Star to show you the path, and appears like a cairn (trail marker), providing clarity at important junctures. "Father" strengthens and emboldens you while holding your unsteady hand in both of his. He is by your side when you take that hesitant first step on a new journey.

Your "Children" appear in everything you tend. They are the first daffodils in springtime. You can see them when kittens play and feel them in the soft tickling of snowflakes melting on your tongue. They are the sliver of a crescent moon, the yeasty smell of bread, about to rise. You can hear your child in the voice of a friend in need, or in the laugh of other children. We tap into their energy when we plant bulbs, or walk dogs, or blow bubbles. If you have ever felt awe while holding a baby, you know about the energy of the universal child.

Your "Lover" continues to love you. Your "Sister" reflects and understands you. Your "Brother" still wants to make you laugh.

Your "Friend" still gets you. Instead of the particular lover, sister, brother, friend, it is the archetypal lover, sister, brother, friend—the timeless, indestructible, and repeating patterns of energy that continue to animate and inform all of us. When we can open up to these presences, we are indeed walking through the world in gratitude, grace, and compassion.

When Death knocks at the door and demands entrance, it is ultimately a call for awareness, deepening, and connection. Nyctea and the Chief reveal some truths about this process, and the steps may be seen as progressive, but also cyclic. We often return, with rawness, to that original pain, or to the despondency of the Abyss. But with each visit there is movement, however subtle. What becomes apparent is that these forays into night consciousness (or complex, uncomfortable feelings) inform our waking life. Earlier, the myth of Persephone was presented as an example of why eating the food of the dead is "tricky business." Another view would be that when Persephone eats the pomegranate seeds and commits herself to six months in the underworld, perhaps she knowingly descends to a place that promotes self-understanding, and she brings those gifts back with her to the upper world each year. Knowledge of the "underworld" adds the necessary shadow for the light, providing dimension to interactions and the capacity to open to the mystery. If integrated, Death can enrich us.

Seeing Death as transformative requires questioning some of our cultural assumptions. One issue to overcome is that in our either/or, dualistic system, Life and Death, Light and Dark, Conscious and Unconscious, Inside and Outside, Self and Other are seen as separate. Not only are they seen as distinct, but there is often a value judgment about one pole being hierarchically better than the other. As an example, we think of Life as being good and Death as being bad. However, in a mythological sensibility they are really one, like two sides of the same coin. Night, Unconsciousness, Shadow, and Death are forgotten or split-off realms of our own worlds. They are within the very fabric of our being, and through grief, being slowly felt, seen and heard—or *recognized*. This recognition paves the way for health.

An exploration of the dark realms and an intimacy with the unknown is one of the fundamental tasks of being human. It is in this place that we are asked to reimagine ourselves within the greater context of the meaningfulness of life. One particularly poignant example of a shift in perspective in the understanding of a life's purpose comes through this story.

Bobsy

When she was healthy, my mother was an absolute angel. She loved her children and grandchildren, and lived for the moments when we would visit. She was so excited to see us that she used to record all of our dinner conversations with a little cassette tape so she could play it over and over again after we left. She would put our pictures out on the mantel so we would feel special. My mother knew what was going on for every child and would listen for hours to their stories. She would collect beautiful agate rocks and slip them into our pockets, whispering that they were good luck charms—the eye of God watching over us. She taught us all what it felt like to be truly loved.

183

Later in her life, she had a series of health issues that really affected her. She broke her ankle, which left her unable to walk. She gained a great deal of weight and was not able to do things for herself anymore. My father became her servant, fetching her coffee and getting her to the toilet. She became increasingly restless and unhappy. Then her arthritis became so bad that she was unable to write letters anymore. This change was really the death of my mother, as her whole identity revolved around being the "glue" in our family, keeping all the cousins connected. She also developed a shooting pain across her stomach, which no doctor seemed to be able to remediate. I watched my mother transform into a demanding and somewhat bitter person. My father worked around the clock to try to keep her comfortable, but it never seemed to be enough.

When she died, it was somewhat of a relief. But, it was still an enormous loss, a Mother-shaped hole in our universe. I was standing by my father at the memorial and I said to him, "You know, Mom was really lucky to have you, you took such good care of her."

My father looked up wisely at me and said, "Oh no, your mother wasn't lucky at all. She was in a tremendous amount of pain, and it was the least I could do to try to help her through it." I was astounded by his grace and felt shaken back to the roots of compassion. Later that day, I sat with my 7-year-old grandson during the reception that followed. He seemed perfectly fine, laughing and playing with his cousins. I knew he had a very special connection with my mother and I was a little worried. I asked him if he was OK. He said, "The reason we are here is to love each other and be kind. Nana already knew how to do that, so her work here was done." With that, he ran back into the yard to play tag with the other kids. I learned so much that day.

⋯◈⋯

Death in some senses, gives us an opportunity to give our full attention to love, to let it teach us, and to realize that we are being offered fullness and relationship in the land of the living and the dead. The experience of loss leads us deeper into the night. And there, it often feels chaotic. In the Greek tradition, Chaos is the genesis of all life. Chaos, in turn, gives birth to Eros (Love), and all the other plants and creatures are born of Eros. In this tradition, Eros is the energy from which we all come, and to which we all return. An awareness of love in the place of loss is one of the things we are tasked with bringing from the depths back to the light of ordinary days. In this gesture we know the true beauty of the erasure of separation and the power of a life animated by Death.

Furthermore, we are not setting out on this road of trials alone. Thirty thousand generations of people have gone before us and created signposts through religion, myth, stories, literature, and science. We only have to pay attention, and many surprising things will emerge. Where we thought we would be afraid, we find ourselves feeling more secure than ever. And where we thought we would lose our identity, we find that we have developed a richer, more defined sense of self. And where we thought we would be most lonely, we find that we are at one with all. Mogenson says, "Mourning is not the process by means of which we let go of human beings. On the contrary, it is the *rite de passage* in which all generations join together to make human beings of one another."[7] This rite of passage offers us a chance to serve Love.

The Tlingit tale ends, "*The woman did not move much and she never spoke. But the Chief knew what the image-woman had to say. It was through his dreams that he knew she was talking to him.*" The story tells us that we are still connected to our individual loved ones. Similarly, Nyctea reminds us of our relationship to the universal. "*And when her song is finished the owl opens its yellow/green eyes, spreads its wings and flies, equipped now to cross the owl's bridge to the next realm, leaving a downy feather or two and the quivering memory of its beauty in the dank, wet air.*" We are being asked to wave goodbye while saying hello.

Love is, indeed, more powerful than Death.

Post Script.

Ram Dass said, "We're all just walking each other home."[8] This wisdom has held me through many significant losses since I sat in the back of that car holding Scot's hand on the way to the mortuary so many years ago. Each time I face a new death, it is like being drop kicked into the Abyss and all the places in between. But through this process, I am learning to let go of two things: an attachment to the physical and my own ego. Death is truly humbling, and I take some consolation in knowing that this book is my way of saying: *I still love.*

---

[7] Greg Mogenson, *Greeting the Angels* (New York: Baywood, 1992), xv.
[8] Ram Dass & Paul Gorman, *How Can I Help?* (New York: Alfred P. Knopf, 1999), 217.

Bibliography

Abraham, Karl. 1924/1949. *Selected Papers on Psychoanalysis.* London: Hogarth.

Andersen, Hans Christian. 1974. "The Snow Queen." In *Hans Christian Andersen, The Complete Tales and Stories.* New York: Anchor.

Asbjørnsen, Peter and Webbe Dasent, George. *East of the Sun and West of the Moon*, 1922. New York: George H. Doran Company, a division of Dover.

Augustus, Kathleen. 2015. "Poem 12." http://www.kaugustus.com.

Barrett, Deirdre. 1992. "Through the Glass Darkly: Images of the Dead in Dreams." *Omega: Journal of Death and Dying, 24,* 97-108.

Bateman, Kimberly. 1999. "The Appearance of the Deceased in Dreams of the Bereaved." *Unpublished doctoral dissertation.* Carpinteria, CA: Pacifica Graduate Institute.

Bateman, Kimberly. 2015. "Symbolmaking in Bereavement: The Temples at Burning Man." In *And Death Shall Have Dominion: Interdisciplinary Perspectives on Dying, Caregivers, Death, Mourning and the Bereaved,* by eds. Malecka, Katarzyna and Gibbs, Rossanna. Oxford: Interdisciplinary.net.

Bettelheim, Bruno. 2010. *The Uses of Enchantment.* New York: Vintage Books.

Blickley, Mark. 2001. "The Pigeon Man Sings." In *Inside Grief*, by ed. Line Wise, 56-59. Incline Village: Wise Press.

Bowlby, John. 1980. *Attachment and Loss: Loss, Sadness and Depression.* New York: Basic Books.

Bowlby, John. 1961. "Process of Mourning." *International Journal of Psychoanalysis 42,* 317-340.

Campbell, Joseph.1973. *The Hero with a Thousand Faces.* Princeton: Princeton University Press.

Chopra, Deepak. 1997. *The Path to Love.* New York: Random House.

Cobain, Rebecca. 2013. "email." Truckee, CA: September 2, 2013.

Crow, Liz. 2001. "A Certain Knowing." In *Inside Grief,* by ed. Line Wise. Incline Village: Wise Press.

Dass, Ram, and Paul Gorman. 1999. *How Can I Help?* New York: Alfred P. Knopf.

Eliade, Mircea. 1987. *The Encyclopedia of Religion.* New York: Routledge.

Fenichel, Otto. 1945. *The Psychoanalytic Theory of Neurosis.* New York: Norton.

Freud, Sigmund. 1917/1959. "Mourning and Melancholia." In *Collected Works, Vol. 4,* by ed. J. Riviere, 154. New York: Basic.

Funk, Colin. 2013. "Moving Stories: the Embodiment of Personal Narrative at Life's End." *Making Sense of Dying and Death.* Athens: Interdisciplinary.net.

Garfield, Patricia. 1997. *The Dream Messenger.* New York: Simon & Schuster.

Gilmore, Lee. n.d. *Burning Man.* Accessed August 26, 2015. http://burningman.org/event/art-performance/playa-art/building-the-temple/.

Gimbutas, Marija. 1991. *The Language of the Goddess.* San Francisco: HarperCollins.

Bibliography

Hedge-Carruthers, Ann. 2016. *unpublished manuscript.* Little Rock, AR.

Holy Bible. King James Version. 1989. Iowa Falls: World Publishing.

Innes, Brian. 1999. *Death and the Afterlife.* New York: St. Martin's.

Johnson, Robert. 1986. *Inner Work.* San Francisco: Harper.

Jung, Carl G. 1947/1969. "The Psychological Aspects of Kore." In *The Collected Works,* by ed. H. Read, 345. Princeton: Princeton University Press.

Jung, Carl G. 1992. in Eds. Rothgeb, Carrie & Clemens, Siegfried. *Abstracts of the Collected Works of C.G. Jung.* Princeton: Princeton University Press.

Kipnis, Aaron. 1994. "Men, Movies, and Monsters: Heroic Masculinity as a Crucible of Male Violence." *Psychological Perspectives: A Quarterly Journal of Jungian Thought, 29, 1,* 38-51.

Kubler-Ross, Elisabeth. 1969. *On Death and Dying.* New York: MacMillan.

Leonard, Linda. 1989. *Witness to the Fire: Creativity and the Veil of Addiction.* Boston: Shambala.

Levine, Stephen, and Ondrea Levine. 1982. *Who Dies?* New York: Anchor Books.

Lindemann, Erik. 1944. "Symptomology and Management of Acute Grief." *American Journal of Psychiatry,* 101: 142.

Ma'Sumian, Frnaz. 1995. *Life After Death: A Study of the Afterlife in World Religions.* Oxford: Oneworld.

Marris, Peter. 1954. *Widows and Their Families.* London: Routledge & Kegan Paul.

Merwin, William S. 1993. "Separation." *The Second Four Books of Poems.* Port Townsend, Washington: Copper Canyon Press.

Mitchell, Ellen, Volpe, Rita, Long, Ariella, Levine, Phyllis, Goldstein, Barbara, Eisenberg, Barbara, Lorenza, Collette, Cohen, Audrey and Barkin, Carol. 2009. *Beyond Tears: Living after Losing a Child.* New York: St. Martin's Griffin.

Mogenson, Greg. 1992. *Greeting the Angels.* New York: Baywood.

Moody, Raymond. 1975/2015. *Life After Life.* New York: Harper-Collins.

Moore, Thomas. 2004. *Dark Nights of the Soul.* New York: Gotham.

Muir, John. 1986. "The Well." *unpublished lecture.* Incline Village, NV.

Ovid. 2010. "Echo and Narcissus." In *Metamorphoses*, by Stanley trans. Lombardo, 79-81. Indianapolis: Hacket.

Parkes, Colin M. 1972. *Bereavement: Studies of Grief in Adult Life.* London: Tavistock.

Parkes, Colin, Pittu Laungani and William Young, eds. 1997. *Death and Bereavement Across Cultures.* New York: Routledge.

Padawer, Estelle. 2001. "Dirge." In *Inside Grief*, by ed. Line Wise, 31. Incline Village: Wise Press.

Pollack, George H. 1961. "Mourning and Adaptation." *International Journal of Psychoanalysis, 42*: 354.

Pollack, George H. 1978. "Process and Affect: Mourning and Grief." *International Journal of Psychoanalysis, 59*: 267.

Pollack, George H. 1989. *The Mourning Liberation Process.* Madison: International University Press.

Pinkola- Estés, Clarissa. 1997. *Women Who Run with the Wolves.* New York: Ballantine.

Raphael, Beverly. 1983. *The Anatomy of Bereavement.* New York: Basic.

Bibliography

Reed, Alexander. 2001. *Aboriginal Myths: Tales of the Dreamtime.* Sydney: Reed New Holland.

Rilke, Rainer Maria. 1973. "Poems from the French." *The American Poetry Review*, 3-3.

Roeder, Stephanie. 1981. "Dreams and Grieving: A Qualitative Exploration of Dreams during the Period of Mourning Following the Death of Parent," *unpublished doctoral dissertation,* Boston University.

Romanyshyn, Robert. 1993. *unpublished lecture.* "Hosting Ghosts" (March 15).

Ronnberg, Ami, and Kathleen, eds. Martin. 2012. *Book of Symbols.* San Francisco: Taschen.

Sanders, Catherine M. 1989. *Grief: The Mourning After: Dealing with Adult Bereavement.* New York: Wiley & Sons.

Schafer, Roy. 1968. *Aspects of Internalization.* New York: Philosophical.

Sesin, Carmen. 2014. *NBC News.* December 29. Accessed August 16, 2015. http://www.nbcnews.com/news/latino/growing-devotion-santa-muerte-u-s-abroad-n275856.

Shigeta Shin'ichi, Gaynor Sekimori and 繁田信一. 2013. "Abe No Seimei." *Japanese Journal of Religious Studies, 40, 1,* 77-97.

Siggins, Lorraine D. 1966. "Mourning: A Critical Survey of the Literature." *International Journal of Psychoanalysis, 47,* 14-25.

Spencer, Anita. 1996. A *Crisis of Spirit: Our Desperate Search for Integrity.* Oklahoma City: Insight Books.

Sullivan, Harry. 1956. "The Dynamics of Emotion." In *Clinical Studies in Psychiatry*, by ed. H.L. Sullivan, Ch. 5. New York: Norton.

Swanton, John R. 1909. "The Image That Came to Life." In Bureau of Ethnology Bulletin, 39, Accessed November 5, 2015. http://www.sacred-texts.com/nam/nw/tmt/tmt065.htm

Taylor, Susan. 2001. "Waving Goodbye and Waving Hello." In *Inside Grief*, by ed. Line Wise, 60-63. Incline Village: Wise Press.

Van de Castle, Robert. 1994. *Our Dreaming Mind*. New York: Ballantine.

von Löwis of Menar, August. 1922. *Finnische und estnische Volksmärchen*. Jena: Eugen Diederichs. Accessed November 1, 2015. http://www.zeno.org/nid/2000784185X

Webmaster. n.d. *Burning Man*. Accessed August 21, 2013. http://www.burningman.com.

Webmaster. n.d. *Native American Indian Owl Legends, Meaning and Symbolism from the Myths of Many Tribes*. Accessed December 12, 2015. http://www.native-languages.org/legends-owl.htm

Weizman, Savine & Kamm, Phylis. 1985. *About Mourning: Support and Guidance for the Bereaved*. New York: Human Sciences.

Whyte, David. 2015. *Consolations*. Langely: Many Rivers Press.